AF719324

DOS MEETS UNIX

Nutshell Handbooks

Concise, down-to-earth guides to selected UNIX topics. Some related books of interest:

UNIX in a Nutshell for System V or Berkeley, *296 or 272 pp.*

This quick-reference guide includes: frequently-used commands and options; shell syntax (*sh* and *csh*); pattern-matching syntax; *vi* and *ex*; *sed* and *awk*; *troff* requests and escapes; *-ms*, *-mm*, and *-me* macros; *tbl*, *eqn* and *pic* syntax; *adb* and *sdb*; *make* and *sccs*.

Learning the vi Editor, *192 pp.*

Complete guide to text editing with *vi*, the full-screen editor available on most UNIX systems. Fifth edition.

Learning the UNIX Operating System, *84 pp.*

If you are new to UNIX, this concise introduction will tell you just what you need to know to get started.

UNIX in a Nutshell for HyperCard, *1.8 MB*

Series of HyperCard stacks for the Mac that contain useful information for Macintosh users of UNIX systems. (Includes free book *Learning the UNIX Operating System.*)

UNIX for FORTRAN Programmers, *264 pp.*

Using UUCP and Usenet, *210 pp.*

!%@:: The Directory of Electronic Mail Addressing & Networks, *438 pp.*

MH & xmh: E-mail for Users and Programmers, *598 pp.*

DOS meets UNIX, *148 pp.*

UNIX Text Processing, *665 pp.*

Contact us for a catalog of all our books or for orders.

O'Reilly & Associates, Inc.

Books That Help People Get More Out of Computers

632 Petaluma Avenue, Sebastopol, CA 95472
(800) 338-6887 · overseas/local (707) 829-0515 · uunet!ora!nuts

DOS MEETS UNIX

A Departmental Computing Perspective

A Nutshell Handbook

By Dale Dougherty and Tim O'Reilly

DOS Meets UNIX
by Dale Dougherty and Tim O'Reilly

Editor: Tim O'Reilly

Copyright © 1990 O'Reilly & Associates, Inc.
All rights reserved.

Printed in the United States of America

Printing History

Oct. 1986:	Initial printing by Prime Computer covered C-Interface and Merge 386 for the Prime EXL 316 system.
Apr. 1988:	First commercial edition; expanded to cover VP/ix and other products.

Please address comments and questions in care of the publisher:

O'Reilly & Associates, Inc.
632 Petaluma Avenue
Sebastopol, CA 95472
800-338-6887
international +1 707-829-0515

UUCP: uunet!ora!nuts
Internet: nuts@ora.uu.com

While every precaution has been taken in the preparation of this book, the publisher takes no responsibility for errors or omissions, or for damages resulting from the use for the information herein.

[*]

[2/91]

Table of Contents

Preface

MS-DOS (referred to throughout this handbook simply as DOS) is an operating system for single-user personal computers, the IBM-PC, XT, AT and compatibles. UNIX is a multi-user operating system for a wide range of computers, from supercomputers to personal computers.

Right off the bat, let us say that this handbook does not attempt to debate whether DOS-based computers are better than UNIX-based computers, or the reverse. What it tries to do is look at DOS and UNIX computing issues in the context of a business computing environment. It offers a departmental computing perspective on DOS and UNIX, intended for managers and users. The question then becomes not which is better, DOS or UNIX, but how the strengths of both systems can be fully utilized in the same computing environment.

We assume that there are two classes of reader who might be interested in this book.

The first is someone who has worked with personal computers and is familiar with DOS. This reader might be ready to consider the limitations of personal computers and begin investigating what a UNIX computer can do to provide new capabilities. Perhaps the reader is unclear what UNIX offers, but wonders what all the noise is about. For this reader, we've tried to present a perspective on what UNIX can offer, as well as a brief tutorial on the UNIX environment. The DOS user might want to read Chapters 1 and 3 before tackling Chapters 2, 4 and 6.

Our second intended audience is an experienced UNIX user who would like access to DOS applications. While this reader may already have an understanding of the benefits of the UNIX environment, he or she will be interested in our discussions of the innovative products that allow DOS and UNIX to coexist on the same system.

The UNIX user may want to skim Chapter 1, and skip Chapter 3 entirely. To make things easier, here's a roadmap to what the book contains.

Chapter One, *DOS, UNIX and Departmental Computing*, examines the computing environment of a group of people, making the point that such an environment cannot be identified wholly with a computer system, an operating system, an application or the needs of any individual user. It looks at the needs of a group of people who use computers for a variety of tasks. It establishes the role of the departmental computer that provides a wide range of services to local users and others who utilize these services from remote systems.

Chapter Two, *Integrating DOS and UNIX*, looks at the different ways in which DOS and UNIX users find themselves sharing systems. It looks at time-honored solutions such as Xenix/DOS disk partitioning and PC terminal-emulation, and introduces several innovative products that provide a greater degree of integration. PC-Interface, PC-NFS, XenixNet and ViaNet give a PC user remote access to a UNIX system, and allow the use of the UNIX system as a file and print server. DOS/UNIX Merge, from Locus Computing Corp., and VP/ix, from Interactive Systems and Phoenix Techologies, both provide the ability to run off-the-shelf DOS applications on a 386-based UNIX system, or indeed to create an entire DOS environment—a "virtual PC" that hides UNIX entirely from the user.

Chapter Three, *Moving From DOS to UNIX*, discusses the differences that concern the user moving from a DOS environment to UNIX. This chapter is intended both for users who move completely to a UNIX-based system and for those who use the products described in this book to gain partial access to UNIX's multi-user, multi-tasking capabilities for print and file services.

Chapter Four, *PC-Interface: The PC in a Larger Context*, demonstrates how users of personal computers can make use of a UNIX departmental computer. It describes shared file access, remote printer sharing, and remote command execution. While this chapter focuses on PC-Interface, it also looks at other DOS-UNIX networking products such as XenixNet and Western Digital's ViaNet.

Chapter Five, *DOS Under UNIX: Hardware Issues*, discusses the differences between DOS and UNIX hardware, and the compatibility issues that users need to be aware of while running DOS applications on a UNIX system with Merge or VP/ix.

Chapter Six, *Merge and VP/ix: The Virtual DOS Environment*, tries to give a feel for what it is actually like to work in the merged DOS and UNIX environment. It demonstrates how Merge and VP/ix can be used to create a complete DOS environment on a UNIX system.

Chapter Seven, *Merge and VP/ix: Running DOS From UNIX*, describes the features of Merge and VP/ix that let you run DOS programs right from the UNIX prompt, even piping data from DOS to UNIX and back, and taking advantage of UNIX's multi-tasking capabilities to run multiple DOS sessions on the same terminal.

Appendix A, *How the Magic Is Accomplished,* is adapted from a *UNIX Review* article by Ken Sarno, VP/ix project manager at INTERACTIVE Systems Corporation. It provides a more technical, in-depth look at the issues covered in Chapter Five.

Appendix B, *Where to Buy,* tells you where you get the various products described in this book. PC-Interface, Merge 286 and Merge 386, and VP/ix are all sold on an OEM basis, and are supported by a variety of of different UNIX systems. We've tried to point you to systems that support these products.

Finally, there's a glossary and an index, to help you sort through the sometimes confusing mass of competing products and features discussed in this book.

In keeping with its subject matter, this book was produced with the DOS program Ventura Publisher, rather than our normal UNIX *troff.* Dale ran Ventura under Merge 286, with Microport System V/AT. Tim worked on a PC running Ventura and a UNIX toolset for DOS called MKS Toolkit.

Acknowledgements

Special thanks to Julie Buckler, Daniel Gilly and Sue Willing of O'Reilly & Associates, Inc. who also made significant contributions to this book, and to Ken Sarno of INTERACTIVE Systems Corporation, for letting us adapt his *UNIX Review* article for Appendix A.

Trademarks

UNIX is a registered trademark of AT&T. Nutshell Handbook is a trademark of O'Reilly & Associates, Inc. Xenix, MS-DOS, XenixNet and Word are registered trademarks of Microsoft Corporation. PC Interface, Merge 286, and Merge 386 are trademarks of Locus Computing Corporation. Lotus and 1-2-3 are registered trademarks of Lotus Development Corp. Intel, followed by any number, is a trademark of Intel Corporation. VisiCalc is a trademark of VisiCorp. Wordstar is a trademark of Micropro International. System V/AT is a trademark of Microport Systems, Inc. VT100, PDP-11 and VAX are trademarks of Digital Equipment Corporation. IBM, PC and PS/2 are trademarks of International Business Machines. Prime EXL 316 is a trademark of Prime Computers, Inc. VP/ix is a trademark of INTERACTIVE Systems Corporation and Phoenix Technologies, Ltd. 386/ix is a trademark of INTERACTIVE Systems Corporation. PageMaker is a registered trademark of

Aldus Corporation. Ventura Publisher is a trademark of Ventura Software, Inc. Macintosh is a trademark of MacIntosh Laboratories and is licensed to Apple Computer. PC/TCP is a trademark of FTP Software, Inc. NFS, PC-NFS and Sun/IPC are trademarks of Sun Microsystems, Inc. MKS Toolkit is a trademark of Mortice Kern Systems, Inc. ORACLE is a trademark of Oracle Corp. Informix is a trademark of Informix Corp. ViaNet is a trademark of Western Digital Corp.

1
DOS, UNIX and Departmental Computing

- *What kinds of computing resources are required for users to work productively?*
- *What is the most effective way to allocate computing resources for a group of people?*
- *How do you satisfy the needs of users who have very different levels of computing experience and involvement?*

These are the questions being addressed by departmental computing solutions. Departmental computing provides a forum for discussing the computing environment that exists for a group of users who work together. Given the diversity of applications and user experience, given the variety of hardware configurations and software programs, how do you provide an integrated computing environment at the departmental level?

A departmental computing solution can help users be more productive by allowing them to share resources and exchange information between different applications. It can also give them the benefit of locally controlled system administration.

DOS (MS-DOS or PC-DOS) was developed by Microsoft Corporation as an operating system for IBM personal computers. The Personal Computer running DOS supports an enormous library of applications software. It also has established a broad user base, many of whom would not otherwise use a computer in their job. Users can be as different as a senior executive or a mailroom clerk. But DOS's orientation as a personal computer operating system has its limitations in an environment where people need to be able to work together in groups.

UNIX was developed by AT&T's Bell Laboratories as a multi-user, multi-tasking operating system. It is now available for a wide range of computers, including microcomputers, minicomputers, mainframes and supercomputers. As a multi-user system that runs on advanced hardware, UNIX provides a powerful computing environment in which many users can work productively. UNIX has many standard facilities for file management, print spooling, communications, batch and background job processing and system administration. In addition, these services can be extended through a local area network to non-UNIX users, whether connected to personal computers or mainframes.

As a departmental computing solution, a UNIX computer offers the chance to migrate users to a richer computing environment. Yet it is also possible to maintain existing PCs that use familiar or specialized applications, while making use of the UNIX system as a file and print server.

From Personal to Departmental Computing

There is no doubt that the personal computer has had a great impact on business computing. It addressed new areas of computing, broadening the number of useful applications and giving users the freedom to tailor a computing environment to their own liking. It was important that an individual user could choose the software he or she needed for the job, and not have to get approval or support from the Data Processing staff.

People who swore they'd never learn to use computers began using them. Mastering the PC became part of the job. As users gained experience, they discovered new ways to benefit from their PC. The personal computer that was bought for word processing could be used for financial analysis, database management and graphics design.

The personal computer provides a "hands-on" computing environment. It encourages each user to control and manage those applications that he or she requires. Users install and maintain software, add new peripherals or expansion options, and do their own troubleshooting.

But the "do-it-yourself" personal computing environment can have its frustrations. Users encounter tedious technical problems that they cannot solve. Neither the support staff of a local computer store nor the in-house DP staff are willing to take complete responsibility for solving these problems.

All I want is to print this memo. But, of course, the printer jams, and I spend fifteen minutes trying to load paper, ten more minutes to find the printer manual, and another half hour to test the suggested remedies. Finally, I end up feeding the paper by hand into the printer, standing there watching while it prints ten pages. What a waste of time! How long would it have taken to type it?

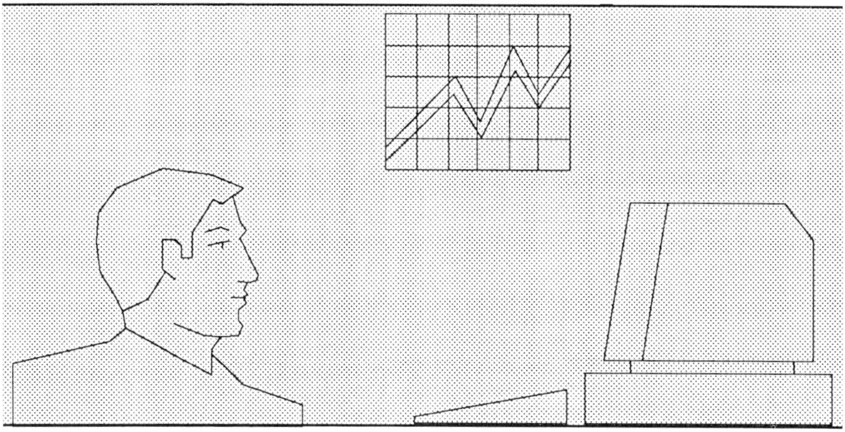

Figure 1-1
"Using a PC effectively has become a big part of my job."

Nothing is ever as simple as it seems, especially if it appears that way in the manual. One might buy a car to drive to and from work. However, the car needs maintenance and parts periodically; collision insurance is required; and you need a driver's license before you can get behind the wheel. Some people feel that the hassle of owning a car is not worth the convenience of driving it. Similarly, some people feel that the frustrations of using a computer cancel out any real gain in productivity.

There is a certain amount of time spent maintaining a computer system. These tasks, such as performing regular backups, become more of a burden for each user. Sometimes, these tasks are ignored, resulting in unexpected disasters. Experienced users soon begin to realize that if they are to continue to be productive, they need more specialized technical support.

This support might cover a range of tasks:

- Daily and Weekly Tape Backup
- Installing and Configuring Software
- Printer Set Up and Operations
- Network Administration
- File Management
- General Troubleshooting

With a larger computer system, these tasks are typically performed by a central DP staff. But should this local group of users depend upon a remote DP staff to solve their problems? If the qualities that define the PC user environment are interactivity and self-reliance, then a centralized approach to managing their computing environment would jeopardize the responsiveness and control that they have enjoyed.

The problem of providing technical support for PC users is just one indication that the computing environment shared by these users needs to be examined. One problem is that the personal computer is like an island in a business computing environment. Each application regards itself as being in complete control over all computing resources. With new applications and new users, the computing environment for each user becomes more complex. Perhaps users are reaching the limits of personal computers, and, more specifically, the limits of DOS.

To be able to work together, users need a more integrated environment than what is offered by strictly "personal" computers. Users need to be able to share files across different systems without passing floppy disks around. They need to share expensive equipment on a departmental, not an individual, basis. For instance, at one time each PC user was content to have an inexpensive dot-matrix printer. Now, if more expensive laser printers, color printers or plotters are to be used, they must be shared by a group of people in order to justify the cost.

A Departmental Computing Solution

A departmental computing solution makes the assumption that a business cannot expect to find a single computer system that will address all the needs of all users. Each computer system must be suited to the needs of its users and the requirements of their applications.

A departmental computing solution creates a distributed processing environment, where a variety of computer systems are supported across a communications network. Distributing processing among multiple computers on a local area network is often a more efficient, less contentious way of getting things done. However, distributed environments vary in the degree of integration that they offer.

One way to create a departmental computing environment is simply by networking personal computers together. A PC network is distributed in the sense that each user has his or her own processor and users can transfer files between machines. But PC networks do not always provide a sufficient level of integration. More importantly, PC networks can only connect a group of similar or identical computers.

A departmental computer system plays a key role in providing an integrated environment at the local level. It is a multi-user computer system that serves as a hub

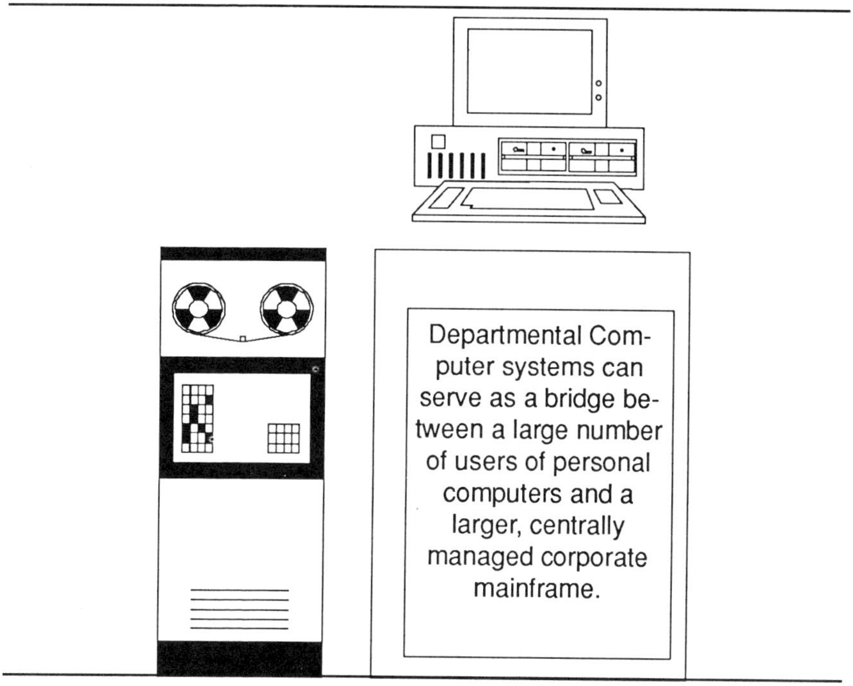

Figure 1-2
Departmental computers in the role of communications bridge.

in a local area network. This network can be extended vertically by connections to mainframe computers or personal computers and horizontally by connections to other departmental-level computer systems. The departmental computer acts like a supervisor, managing and overseeing resources and operations common to all users.

Once such an integrated solution has been implemented, a terminal might replace the personal computer on the desk of some users. If personal computers and workstations are dedicated to specialized or processor-intensive applications, these systems could remain self-standing while using the network for file and print services.

For instance, a corporate communications specialist may use desktop publishing software like PageMaker or Ventura Publisher to create newsletters and brochures. This type of application is processor-intensive, requiring a computer system with graphics capabilities. In addition, a laser printer is an essential part of running this application.

The specialist's computing needs might be different from others in the department. Others produce letters and reports with a word processing package that is not nearly as complicated as PageMaker. They don't need any graphics hardware to run their applications. However, these users would like to have access to the laser printer.

In turn, it would be very useful if everyone could share files. For instance, the communications specialist might receive the copy for a brochure from a co-worker, who has entered it in a WordStar file. Similarly, others in the department are often working on joint projects where access to the same body of information is important, especially if the information is changing rapidly.

To implement this type of departmental computing solution, a central machine that acts as a file server is essential. Without a file server, the department might produce multiple copies of the same file, and some of these copies might get out-of-sync with other copies. A file server provides a central storage location for important files and ensures that users have access to a single, correct copy.

So, in this department scenario, the communications specialist might keep her PC for PageMaker, while her co-workers might give up their PCs and use terminals connected to the UNIX system. As you'll see later on, with additional software, users who have moved from a DOS to a UNIX environment can still have access to familiar DOS applications.

A Departmental Computer System

A departmental computer system can be considered as a bridge between personal computing, where individual users are left to their own devices, and corporate computing, where very large computers are administered in a central location by a highly specialized technical staff. A departmental computer system is able to address user needs in ways that personal computers and mainframe computers cannot.

A departmental computer must be versatile. It has to provide:

- A platform for multi-user applications such as database management, word processing and communications.
- Centralized data storage, providing facilities for file security, file system backup, and distributed user access.
- A server for multiple printers, modems, and terminals.

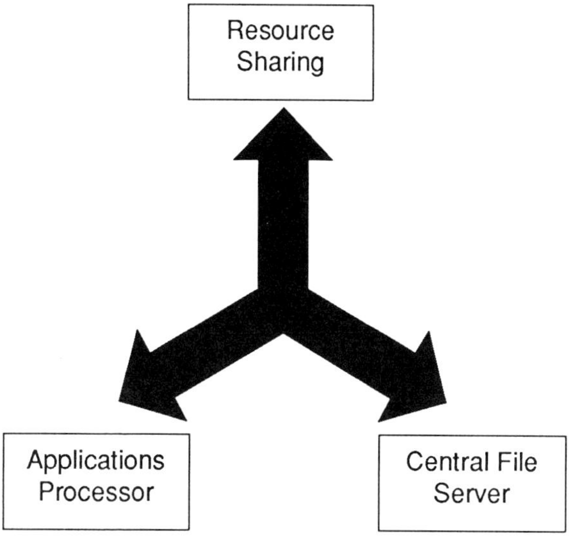

Figure 1-3
Roles performed by a departmental computer.

Mid-range UNIX systems offer the performance and functionality required of a departmental computer. Traditionally, these mid-range systems have been called minicomputers. Recently, a new system classification has emerged, the *super-microcomputer*. These systems include new Intel 80386-based machines by Prime Computer and Convergent Technologies and established Motorola 68020-based machines such as the NCR Tower series. Typically, they are 32-bit machines that support anywhere from 8 to 80 users.

(In addition, there is a class of high-powered technical workstations, typified by those offered by Sun Microsystems. While technically multi-user systems, workstations tend to be dedicated to a single user running compute-intensive graphics applications. Multiple workstations can be networked together to create a seamless computing environment for multiple users—but that is somewhat beyond the scope of our discussion, which focusses on standard multi-user UNIX machines.)

Support for industry standards has been a common theme in the demand for and the design of minicomputers and supermicrocomputers. Instead of purchasing all equipment and software from a single vendor, a buyer can choose from a range of suppliers, many of whom are offering very similar products.

The Benefits of UNIX

The UNIX operating system has become a de facto industry standard for multi-user computer systems, largely because of its portability across a wide range of computer configurations. We'll discuss what this means and why it influences the decision to choose a UNIX system.

In addition, we'll discuss UNIX's facilities for system administration, file management, print spooling, communications, batch and background job processing and as an applications processor.

De Facto Industry Standard

Before such a standard evolved, each computer manufacturer developed a proprietary operating system designed to run on proprietary hardware. The consequence of this approach was that customers were bound to that manufacturer's hardware offerings and were also limited by the software that manufacturer supported.

By supporting UNIX, instead of a proprietary operating system, customers and manufacturers can both benefit. Customers can follow the UNIX manufacturers who are able to present them with the most advanced hardware, without jeopardizing the viability of their software investment. Manufacturers can develop and introduce new hardware technology at a faster rate, without having to wait for the development of a proprietary operating system.

Portability

One of the main benefits of the UNIX operating system is its portability. It runs on a number of very different hardware architectures built by a variety of manufacturers. DOS, on the other hand, is limited to a specific hardware configuration, the personal computer as established by IBM. For instance, DOS and UNIX can run on systems based on Intel 8086, 80286, and 80386 chips; UNIX can also run on Motorola 68000- and 68020-based systems, and on systems that use proprietary chips.

Portability makes UNIX an attractive platform for multi-user applications. As the hardware technology continues to improve, applications can be easily moved to new hardware to realize better performance.

Multi-User Applications

While the number of business applications for UNIX systems as compared to DOS systems is relatively small, these numbers are increasing significantly. Often resembling their DOS cousins, these applications offer the additional resources of a UNIX system for word processing, speadsheets, graphics, project management, and database mangement. Among the leading applications are multi-user database products such as Oracle and Informix.

In addition, the 32-bit addressing on 80386 and 68000 UNIX machines supports large, powerful applications (e.g., AI inference engines) that are just too big for DOS.

File Management

UNIX supports a hierarchical file system, similar to DOS. Each user has his or her own home directory on the file system, but can access files anywhere on the system.

File security is an important issue in a multi-user environment. Each user is given an account with a unique login id, so his or her identity is always known to the system. Users can specify file permissions that determine who can access and modify their files. These permissions can be set to allow access only to the file's owner, to members of a predefined group of users, or to all users.

Printer Services

UNIX provides a print spooler, a program that allows all users to share one or more printers. A spooler keeps track of print requests and passes jobs to the printer on a first-come, first-served basis. A user can make a printing request at any time, even if the printer is currently busy. Requests are queued and processed in order as the printer becomes available.

Communications

Another strength of the UNIX environment is communications and networking. This is not much of a surprise, given that UNIX was developed at AT&T's Bell Labs. Even at an early stage in its development, UNIX has provided standard utilities for electronic mail, remote login, file transfer and remote command execution.

The standard UNIX communications facility is UUCP (UNIX-to-UNIX copy), which can establish a store-and-forward network between UNIX systems. UUCP is used both for file transfer and to facilitate the transport of electronic mail.

Electronic mail is one of the most visible benefits of a multi-user system. New UNIX users quickly come to rely on their ability to forward messages to other users on the same system, as well as to other systems connected in a worldwide UUCP network.

Most UNIX systems also support an Ethernet networking capability and a variety of communications protocols. Sun's Network File System (NFS) has been adopted by a great many UNIX system manufacturers (as well as by manufacturers of other types of systems, including supercomputers). NFS supports transparent access to files distributed across a network. AT&T's most recent release (System V Release 3) supports a similar facility called RFS (Remote File System). These facilities allow users to access remote files transparently, as if the files were located on the local system.

In addition, networking software provided by manufacturers or third-party developers can extend these services through a local area network to remote users, whether connected to personal computers or mainframes. Several programs that we look at in the next chapter, PC-Interface and Merge/386 from Locus Computing, and VP/ix from Interactive Systems and Phoenix Technologies, create a high level of integration between the DOS and UNIX environments. These products help overcome one major weakness of UNIX relative to DOS, its lack of off-the-shelf applications.

Multi-tasking

In DOS, each program is executed as a single task on a dedicated processor. The user must wait for one task to finish before starting another one. Multi-tasking is the ability to execute multiple tasks by having them share time on the processor. UNIX manages the allocation of processor time so that these multiple tasks can run concurrently.

Multi-tasking also allows each user to run multiple programs. For instance, you can run a slow number-crunching program in the background while continuing to work interactively in the foreground. Background processing is useful for long-running programs whose output does not need to be monitored immediately. Once you enter a command that places a program in the background, the system prompt returns, and you can enter another command. Using Merge or VP/ix, it is now possible to multi-task DOS applications.

Another feature of the UNIX multi-tasking environment is the ability to specify commands that will be run automatically at a later time. A system administrator can request that UNIX perform some task every day at a certain time. These are tasks invoked by the *cron* facility. For instance, a UUCP request might be executed nightly to transfer files over long-distance phone lines when off-peak rates are in effect.

System Administration

Most of what UNIX is doing is done behind the scenes. The user does not need to get involved. At most installations, a single person will be designated the system administrator.

The administrator is really a system resource shared by all users. The frustrating problems associated with computer use often result from the fact that nobody can put in the time to troubleshoot these unexpected problems. In these situations, an administrator can be a godsend.

A UNIX system requires some administration. The tasks are not difficult to perform, but someone must be responsible for them. The administrator will perform a variety of tasks for all users, including setting up new accounts, backup of user and system files, and configuring new devices such as printers and terminals. UNIX provides a number of utilities that make it easier to manage the computing resources for a group of users.

Program Development

UNIX provides an excellent program development environment. It includes many tools for designing, implementing and maintaining software programs. In particular, it is well-suited to program development projects that require the efforts of a team of people.

C is the programming language of UNIX. Standard utilities for compiling, linking and debugging C programs are provided. A library of system calls is used to access the operating system directly. There are UNIX system calls for opening and closing files, scheduling and monitoring processes, and others that allocate system resources. In the most recent UNIX release, System V Release 3, UNIX has added file and record locking and special facilities for building distributed applications.

In Conclusion

The UNIX facilities described in this book provide the flexibility to expand the scope of the departmental computing environment. The next chapter takes a look at some specific ways to integrate DOS and UNIX operating environments.

2
Integrating DOS and UNIX

This chapter looks at different ways of integrating DOS and UNIX in a departmental computing environment.

The basic options for integrating DOS and UNIX include:

1. Setting up a communications link between a PC and a UNIX system, and using a terminal emulation program to log in to the UNIX host. This option allows you to transfer files between the two environments.

2. Using the UNIX system as a file and print server for networked PCs. Products such as PC-Interface and PC-NFS give the user direct access to files and devices in the UNIX environment. In addition, the PC user can execute commands on the UNIX system and capture the output in the DOS environment.

3. Running DOS and UNIX concurrently on a multi-user system. This might involve using a co-processor board like the SunIPC (Integrated Personal Computer) for Sun Workstations, or more likely, using one of the new software products, DOS/UNIX Merge or VP/ix, that allows full integration of DOS and UNIX on an Intel 80386 processor.

A departmental computing solution might involve all three levels of integration.

Note: This chapter introduces several software products that offer different levels of DOS/integrating with UNIX. Although we discuss departmental computing solutions in terms of software, remember that your choices are also very much hardware-oriented. For example, selecting a product like PC-Interface or PC-NFS lets you use networking connections to preserve your existing investment in PC hardware. Merge, on the other hand, runs only on an 80286- or 80386-based system, but it may let you replace individual PCs with low-cost terminals. Sun Microsystems' SunIPC runs DOS applications on a Sun

Workstation, which has a Macintosh-like interface with icons and a mouse.

Connecting to a UNIX Host

There are several ways of physically connecting personal computers and UNIX systems in a local area network. Two of the most popular are:

- RS-232 serial connection
- Ethernet high-speed connection

You can use an RS-232 serial cable to connect a PC to a UNIX host, just as you can connect terminals to UNIX. A serial cable is a low-cost connection.

An Ethernet connection requires an Ethernet controller on both ends. Ethernet boards for PCs are supplied by manufacturers such as 3Com, Micom-Interlan, and Excelan, and plug into the PC backplane. For the UNIX host, an Ethernet controller is usually offered as an option by the manufacturer. Each system is connected to an external transceiver, which then connects to the Ethernet cable.

The speed of accessing files on the UNIX host over a communications link depends on whether you have an RS-232 connection or an Ethernet connection. RS-232 connections generally run at a speed of 1200 to 9600 bps (bits per second). Ethernet runs at 10 Mbps (Megabits per second) with the bandwidth shared between all systems and devices on the network. The difference in access time is similar to that between accessing a file on a floppy disk and a file on a hard disk.

If you are not physically close to the UNIX host, you can also use a modem. You can dial up a remote UNIX system and communicate with it over the telephone lines.

Using a Terminal Emulator

After you physically connect a personal computer to a UNIX host, you can use a terminal emulation program to make the PC act like a terminal. A DOS user can log on to the UNIX machine from his or her PC, just as a UNIX user can log on from a terminal.

There are a large number of commercial and public-domain communications programs that can be used over an RS-232 or telephone link to turn a PC into a terminal on a UNIX system. However, our favorite is a product called TERM, from

Century Software in Salt Lake City. Unlike most PC communications programs, TERM is also available in a UNIX implementation.

During a login session, the PC user has complete access to UNIX facilities but can "escape" to the local DOS level to execute commands. File transfer between UNIX and DOS is also provided. It is in this area that TERM exceeds its competition. Because the same communications program is running on both ends, it is possible to perform error-checked file transfers. (UNIX systems do not usually support xmodem and other protocols often used for file transfers between PCs.)

Furthermore, TERM includes a powerful script language, and a variety of predefined scripts that can simulate the action of a local area network. For example, it is not necessary to actually log in to transfer files or to execute batch commands on the UNIX system—the DOS user can simply issue a local command to copy a file between DOS and UNIX, or to send a file to a printer on the UNIX system.

However, the user remains very much aware of the boundaries of two very distinct systems. Files are not truly shared—they are simply copied between systems. And because the PC is a single-tasking system, transferring large numbers of files can be a tedious operation—the kind of thing you start before heading out for coffee.

In addition, terminal emulation does not provide centralized backup of DOS files, and allows only limited access to remote devices from the DOS environment. And of course, the flow of information is completely under the control of the PC user. For all practical purposes, access to files on the DOS system by other UNIX users is impossible.

Finally, the DOS user gets the benefit of UNIX's multi-tasking features only by switching, at least part time, to the UNIX environment.

Nonetheless, in a departmental computing environment, terminal emulation can be used in various ways. It can give PC users access to UNIX utilities or it can transform an unused but available PC into a UNIX terminal. And if the chief objective is to give UNIX users access to DOS applications, it may be the preferred alternative. PCs are now nearly as cheap as terminals, and can be used with any existing UNIX system with only a minimal investment in cabling and communications software. Users can switch between the local PC and the UNIX login session at the press of a single key.

TCP/IP Networking Utilities

For PCs connected to a UNIX host via an Ethernet local area network, there is another alternative to consider, namely a PC implementation of the standard TCP/IP networking utilities.

The TCP/IP network protocol and associated utilities were originally developed by DARPA (the Defense Advanced Research Products Agency), and are currently used to connect thousands of academic and research institutions into a network called the ARPA-Internet. TCP/IP has become the standard protocol for Ethernet local area networks, and is sure to be available on any system that supports an Ethernet option. A PC implementation called PC/TCP is available from FTP Software in Cambridge, MA.

The TCP/IP utilities include **telnet** and **rlogin** for terminal emulation, **ftp** and **rcp** for file transfer, and **lpr** for remote printing.

In addition to the greater speed of an Ethernet connection, PC/TCP provides a number of capabilities not found with any serial-port-based communications program. Most importantly, the PC is able to act as a network "server" as well as a "client." That means that it is possible for users on the UNIX system to initiate file transfers to the PC, or to use a printer attached to the PC. In addition, PC/TCP includes a UNIX-compatible mail utility, which means that the PC user can send and receive electronic mail without logging in to the UNIX system.

Still, PC/TCP shares many of the same drawbacks as serial communications programs like TERM. You are still talking about exchanging data between two separate systems, and working in two separate environments in order to get the benefits of each.

PC-Interface and PC-NFS

PC-Interface (Locus Computing Corp.) and Sun's PC-NFS (developed from PC-Interface code) are two products that provide a higher level of integration between DOS and UNIX systems than communications programs do. These programs allow DOS users to access files and devices on a remote UNIX system as easily as they can access those on their own PC.

Both of these products rely on an Ethernet connection between the PC and the UNIX system as the underlying communications link. (Some implementations of PC-Interface can use a serial connection, or local area networks such as Starlan or

Token-Ring.) However, they go far beyond the standard TCP/IP networking utilities in the level of connection between DOS and UNIX systems that they provide.

PC-NFS was built on top of an early version of PC-Interface, and has substantially similar capabilities as a file and print server. PC-Interface has more powerful facilities for remotely executing UNIX commands and applying them to files residing on the local PC. However, PC-NFS allows a PC to connect not only to UNIX systems, but to many different types of systems (including DEC VAXes running VMS and Cray supercomputers), running Sun's Network File System (NFS). PC-NFS is a clear choice if you want to connect to an existing NFS installation consisting of multiple operating systems and mixed hardware.

(As will be discussed in Chapter 4, there are several other DOS/UNIX products with similar capabilities, including XenixNet and ViaNet. However, for purposes of this discussion, we've chosen to focus on PC-Interface and PC-NFS.)

PC-Interface and PC-NFS File Services

To enable file sharing, PC-Interface and PC-NFS establish the UNIX file system as a "virtual drive" on the PC. This virtual drive functions as a channel from the DOS environment to the UNIX environment. That is, the UNIX file system appears to the PC as drive D:. Files residing on the remote UNIX host can be accessed as though they were on a local fixed disk on the PC. You can copy a file to or from the virtual drive just as you would copy it to or from a floppy in the A: drive.

In short, PC-Interface and PC-NFS offer *file access*, as opposed to the *file transfer* facilities that come with a serial communications program or a standard Ethernet connection.

File transfer involves sending a copy of a file from one place to another. While file transfer does allow users to exchange information, it provides no central administration of stored data. In fact, file transfer is just an automated way to walk over to someone else's desk and hand them a file on a floppy disk.

File access, on the other hand, allows users to operate on a single remote file without having to move a copy of that file to their local system. This method of file sharing has many advantages. Since there is only one existing copy of a file, users can avoid the confusion that can occur when more than one person is working on a project, and two of them end up making changes to multiple copies of the same file. Furthermore, files can easily be backed up by a system administrator.

Under PC-Interface and PC-NFS, files stored on the PC's virtual disk (really the UNIX file system) can be accessed by other users, either from terminals connected to the UNIX system, or from other PCs connected with PC-Interface or PC-NFS. Of course, in order to preserve the security required on a multi-user system, all files on the virtual disk are protected by file access permissions, just like native UNIX files.

Perhaps even more exciting is the fact that DOS applications can also be stored on the UNIX disk and accessed from the PC just as if they were resident on a local floppy or fixed disk. Furthermore, PC users can use UNIX files for DOS applications. For instance, a PC user could access information stored in a multi-user database management system.

A small complication is that the file naming conventions and file formats in UNIX and DOS differ slightly. There are software features that compensate for these differences, however. For more information, see Chapter 4.

PC-Interface and PC-NFS also include a simple terminal emulator, so that DOS users can also log in directly to the UNIX system.

One limitation of PC-Interface and PC-NFS is that these programs provide a client-only connection for a PC. In other words, the PC user can access UNIX files, but UNIX users cannot directly access DOS files on the PC's own disk drives. Of course, as mentioned earlier, the PC user can copy DOS files to the virtual drive on the UNIX file system and thus share them with other users.

PC-Interface and PC-NFS Print Services

PC-Interface and PC-NFS allow you to use a local printer connected to the PC or a remote printer connected to a UNIX system. You can establish either a local or a remote printer as the default printer for a working session. Using a local printer is done as it is normally done in DOS, by directing output to one of the LPT channels. You associate a remote printer with the PC by logically mapping it to a DOS communications port. This means that the remote printer can be accessed from within DOS applications without any special setup.

PC-Interface Remote Command Execution

Using PC-Interface, a PC user can execute commands on the remote UNIX system. However, the implementation of this feature is so transparent that the user

UNIX Tools for DOS

There are several companies that provide DOS versions of UNIX tools. These programs, of course, run entirely under DOS.

For instance, you can buy an MS-DOS implementation of **vi**, the UNIX full-screen text editor. Since **vi** is interactive, you could otherwise run this program only from a terminal emulator, not with a product like PC-Interface's ON utilities. Having a general purpose tool such as a full-screen editor improves the flexibility of DOS immensely.

Many of the unique tools found in the UNIX environment are intended for programmers. As C gained popularity in non-UNIX environments, such as MS-DOS, the manufacturers of C compilers also shipped their own versions of UNIX-like programming tools. Thus, you can find a version of **make** and **SCCS** that will run on DOS.

The MKS Toolkit is the best example of expanding the DOS environment with UNIX tools. It provides versions of many popular UNIX utilities, such as **grep**, **sed**, **awk**, **cpio** and **ls**. The MKS Toolkit even provides the Bourne shell and the Korn Shell, which can replace COMMAND.COM as the DOS command interpreter.

Running UNIX tools under DOS provides some of the benefits of fully integrating the two worlds, in that the PC user can work in a richer environment. However, like disk partitioning, this is a limited solution. The PC user is still not part of the multi-user UNIX environment and cannot share DOS files with UNIX users.

thinks he or she has simply expanded the utilities available in the DOS environment.

PC-Interface's ON utilities allow a DOS user to run the non-interactive stream-oriented commands of the UNIX environment on DOS files. The output from a command can then be redirected to other DOS or UNIX commands. These utilities give a DOS user versatile tools for manipulating existing data on the PC.

(Of course, there are also low-cost implementations of UNIX tools that can be run directly on DOS systems. For more information, see the sidebar *UNIX Tools for DOS*.)

In Summary

PC-Interface and PC-NFS provide a high level of integration between DOS and UNIX. They allow a department to preserve an investment in PC hardware and broaden the range of tools and devices available to PC users. In particular, they extend the usefulness of floppy-only PCs by providing access to central disk storage.

In addition, PC-Interface and PC-NFS allow for centralized backup of PC files.

These two solutions do a lot to bring UNIX to DOS, but are more limited in bringing DOS to UNIX. Although UNIX users can be given access to DOS files, they cannot run DOS application software, except from a connected PC.

Dual Operating Environments

Intel-based microprocessors can support both UNIX and DOS environments. This means that DOS and UNIX can reside on the same machine, using the same microprocessor. In the following sections, we look at four different ways of providing dual operating environments.

- Disk partitioning
- DOS hardware co-processors such as SunIPC
- DOS software emulators such as SoftPC
- Merge and VP/ix

Disk Partitioning

Systems that are based on the Intel 8086, 80286 or 80386 microprocessors can run either the DOS or UNIX operating systems. It's easy enough to use both operating systems on the same machine by partitioning the hard disk. DOS resides on one partition and UNIX or Xenix resides on the other. One of these operating systems resides in the boot partition and is the default operating system; it runs when the system is powered on. The alternate operating system must be booted from a floppy disk.

How the Chips Stack Up

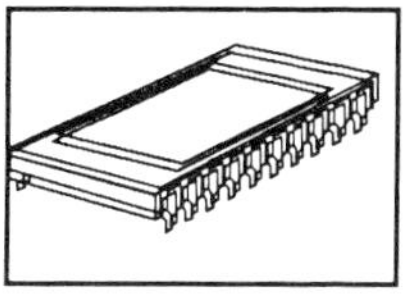

The Intel 8086 is the microprocessor chip at the heart of the IBM Personal Computer. The 80286 is a more powerful chip used to develop a more powerful personal computer, the IBM PC/AT. Both of these computers use 16-bit architectures. The 80386 is the newest Intel chip. Although it can be used in an IBM PC/AT, it is the first of this family specifically designed for 32-bit architectures.

A unique feature of the Intel chips is their upward compatibility. The 80286 and the 80386 are able to run applications that were designed for the 8086.

The 80386 has three modes of operation, two of which provide protected environments for 8086 and 80286 applications, respectively. Its native mode is 32-bit.

The unique architecture of 80386 is designed for a product like Locus Computing Corp.'s Merge or Interactive's VP/ix. This allows DOS applications to run concurrently on the same microprocessor with UNIX.

The other popular chip is the 68000 series by Motorola. The 68000, 68010, and 68020 are used in many UNIX machines and graphics-oriented computers, such as the Apple Macintosh and the Commodore Amiga. Motorola's yet to be released 68030 is expected to exceed Intel's 80386 in power, but lacks the ability to run DOS applications.

The industry is examining and debating the most recent chips produced by Intel and Motorola, the 80386 and the 68030.

Partitioning a PC's disk basically gives you two operating systems for one machine. However, you cannot go from one environment to the other without rebooting the machine.

In addition, there is only limited interchange between the two operating systems. While in DOS, you can't access a file in the UNIX partition. However, from the UNIX side, there are a few utilities you can use to access DOS files. In Xenix, Microport System V/AT, and Interactive Systems' 386/ix, there are special utilities that allow you to list and copy DOS files and directories on the DOS partition, as well as on DOS-formatted disks in the floppy drive.

Disk partitioning can be used to transform a PC-class machine into an inexpensive UNIX system. However, this solution does not integrate a PC into a multi-user UNIX environment.

DOS Hardware Co-Processors

For UNIX users who want access to DOS applications, several manufacturers have offered 8086- or 80286-based DOS co-processor boards for their UNIX systems. One such product is the "Integrated Personal Computer" (SunIPC) developed by Sun Microsystems. SunIPC lets the user open a window on a (UNIX-based) Sun workstation and run DOS application software. In addition, other Sun workstations can share this resource by accessing a remote SunIPC board over the network.

Like PC-Interface and PC-NFS, SunIPC provides utilities to convert DOS files to UNIX file format and vice versa. SunIPC also lets you use a Sun Workstation mouse as a PC mouse for DOS application software, and lets a Sun Workstation keyboard emulate an IBM PC keyboard. SunIPC provides both monochrome and color graphics screens for the DOS window, which gives users great flexibility in running DOS applications that make extensive use of graphics.

Obviously, a product like SunIPC does not provide a general solution to the problem of integrating DOS and UNIX. However, it succeeds admirably in making DOS applications available to existing UNIX users.

Emulating DOS in Software

Over the years, a number of companies have offered software products that emulate DOS on processors other than the Intel 8086 family. These products have not enjoyed wide acceptance because the overhead of translating 8086 instructions for another processor made these products slow and unwieldy.

As more powerful processors such as the 68020 have become available, the performance of software emulators has become more acceptable. A product recently introduced for the Macintosh II, SoftPC from Insignia Solutions, is making another stab at making software emulation an acceptable answer to running DOS under UNIX. For more information, see the sidebar *Buying a Macintosh II? Consider SoftPC*, in Chapter 5.

Merge and VP/ix

The developers of PC-Interface, Locus Computing Corp., have created a product that uses the unique architecture of the Intel 80386 chip to permit concurrent DOS and UNIX environments that run on a UNIX system. A similar product called VP/ix has been developed by Interactive Systems and Phoenix Technologies. Unlike software emulators, these products actually run both DOS and UNIX on the same processor.

Both of these products are mostly sold on an OEM basis, which means that the choice of which one to use will depend on which one is supplied by your UNIX system vendor. (VP/ix is also sold with Interactive's own implementation of UNIX for the 386, which goes by the name of 386/ix.) Contact Locus or Interactive at the addresses shown in Appendix B for a list of UNIX vendors that support these products.

While either of these products can run on a high-end PC, their real beauty is that they allow a true multi-user computer to run DOS applications. While PC-Interface allows a PC to use the UNIX file system as a virtual disk, these products create an entire "virtual PC" on the UNIX system.

This means that a user doesn't need a PC to run popular DOS programs, such as WordStar and Lotus 1-2-3. They can be stored on the UNIX disk, and used from any terminal connected to the system.

It also means that a DOS-trained user does not have to work in the UNIX environment. With Merge or VP/ix, users have the option of creating and maintaining a DOS environment for all or part of a login session, or creating a DOS environment to run a particular application. Among the DOS applications that run under Merge and VP/ix are popular spreadsheet programs such as Lotus 1-2-3, VisiCalc and Multiplan, and word processors such as WordStar, Word, and Word Perfect.

While in the DOS environment, users have access to UNIX commands and files. Similarly, a UNIX user can freely access DOS utilities and files while retaining the advantages of the multi-tasking UNIX environment. For instance, Merge or VP/ix users can run DOS commands in the background, and can run multiple DOS and UNIX programs concurrently.

With DOS applications running concurrently with UNIX, users who are comfortable in DOS can be moved to a multi-user departmental computing system. These users can then make a gradual transition to UNIX.

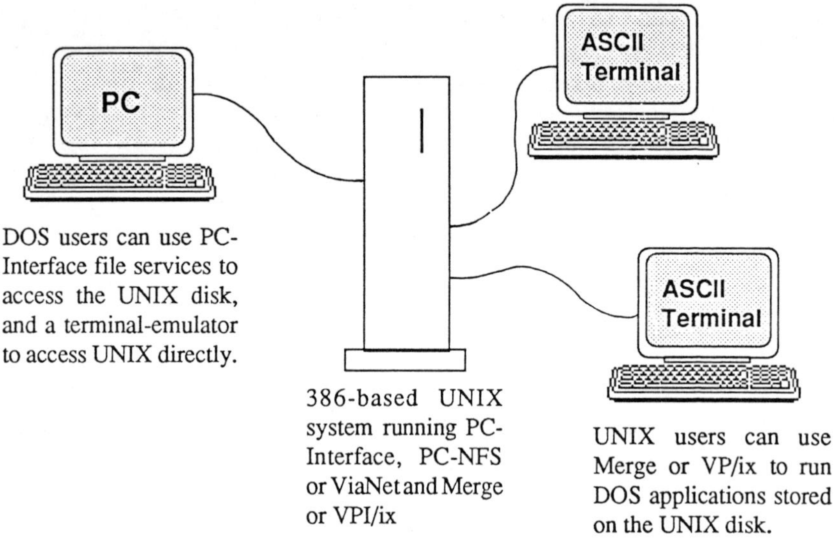

Figure 2-1
A network supporting both DOS and UNIX users.

In Conclusion

- Communications solutions like terminal-emulation and file transfer allow DOS users to log in to the UNIX system, as well as to send files back and forth. The systems remain separate, but users can have access to both environments.

- PC-Interface and PC-NFS (as well as other products like ViaNet and XenixNet) allow DOS users to experience many of the benefits of UNIX without ever “leaving” the PC. The UNIX disk is treated as if it were an extension of DOS. PC-Interface’s ON utilities allow the DOS user to use UNIX utilities as well. However, UNIX system users have no access to DOS.

- Merge and VP/ix allow UNIX users to run DOS, and DOS users to run UNIX. The two environments coexist on the same machine at the same time. No PC may be attached to the system at all—UNIX users may run DOS programs on ASCII terminals.

These three solutions are not exclusive. A PC connected to a UNIX system can use PC-Interface's terminal emulator to log in to the UNIX system, or can use PC-Interface host file services to access the UNIX disk and to store DOS programs on it. UNIX users with standard ASCII terminals can then use Merge or VP/ix to run those programs on the UNIX system.

3
Moving From DOS to UNIX

This chapter presents a discussion of the similarities and differences between DOS and UNIX. It is intended for DOS users who plan to start using a UNIX system. You might be a user accessing UNIX from a PC, using a communications package like TERM or the terminal emulator built into PC-Interface. You might actually be a former DOS user now working on a UNIX system.

Anyone familiar with DOS should not find UNIX perplexing. DOS has a subset of features of the UNIX operating system. Most of the functions that you perform in DOS can be performed in UNIX, often with very similar commands. In fact, a DOS user has a headstart in learning UNIX and can begin working productively in the UNIX environment almost immediately.

Some people feel that UNIX is too difficult for users, when compared to DOS. But it is hardly fair to compare these systems. A task that can be done by a single person is different from one that requires a group of people to work in concert. UNIX is different because it creates a multi-user environment. Certainly, you would not find UNIX any more or less difficult to use, if compared to other multi-user operating systems (many of which at some stage derived features from UNIX).

This chapter has a dual purpose: to lead you to aspects of UNIX that will seem familiar to you and to introduce some of its features that are new to you. Many of these new features will provide you with new capabilities, allowing you to accomplish tasks in UNIX that you could not do in DOS.

One disclaimer before beginning: this chapter is not meant to serve as or replace an introductory UNIX text. Another Nutshell Handbook, *Learning the UNIX Operating System*, is a useful introduction. You should also have access to UNIX documentation if you are going to work in the UNIX environment on a daily basis.

Versions of UNIX

There are several different versions of UNIX. The three main variants are System V, the official version from AT&T, 4*x*BSD (the Berkeley Software Distribution, version 4.2 or 4.3), and MicroSoft Xenix.

System V is commonly found on commercially-oriented UNIX systems; 4.*x*BSD on scientific systems, and Xenix on microcomputers. However, the current version of Xenix is based on System V, and many manufacturers offer hybrid systems with features borrowed from both System V and 4.*x*BSD. In addition, there is a movement to write all these separate versions. By 1990, there should be a single, unified UNIX standard.

Because of legal restrictions on the use of the name UNIX, no one except AT&T and the University of California can actually call their UNIX implementations "UNIX." This is the reason you see names like Xenix, HP-UX, Ultrix, and so on. However, don't be confused—all of these products are really just versions of UNIX.

There are also a number of UNIX "work alikes"—which are not licensed UNIX implementations, but imitate it closely. The most significant of these, in the long run, is GNU (a charming, recursive acronym that stands for **G**nu is **N**ot **U**nix), a public domain UNIX implementation currently under development by the Free Software Foundation.

For the most part, the differences between these systems are not of major importance to the new user. However, we will point out some of the most significant differences in the course of this chapter.

The UNIX Guru

One of the popular myths that surrounds UNIX is that of the guru. The UNIX guru has typically spent most of his academic and professional life contemplating the UNIX operating system. Supposedly, every UNIX system requires a guru, just as a limousine requires a chauffeur. The myth of the UNIX guru contributes to the perception that UNIX is too complex for mere mortals to use.

The existence of this myth can probably be attributed to UNIX's long gestation period in research labs and universities. There are specialists who read UNIX source code and comprehend all the complexity of UNIX. These people are valuable resources in the UNIX community. However, you do not have to be, or aspire to be, a guru to tackle UNIX. While no one disputes that UNIX is more complex than DOS, it is comprehensible and you can choose a level of understanding appropriate to your use.

We don't wish to dispel the myth entirely, though. One question to ask is: if there are UNIX gurus, what has so held their interest?

At the core of UNIX is a design philosophy that is simple and elegant. UNIX provides a number of individual tools, or programs that can be combined in various ways to create new programs that perform specific tasks. Experienced users have confidence that whatever they want to do, they can discover a way to do it in UNIX.

Because a group of users are sharing the system, each user can benefit from the knowledge and efforts of other users. More experienced users might build tools that help less experienced people. The presence of experienced users can make it easier to learn UNIX, especially when you need help troubleshooting a particular problem.

The UNIX Environment

UNIX provides each user with a computing environment in which a number of common tasks can be performed. This computing environment is richer than DOS; quite simply, it provides more standard equipment.

From a user's point of view, there are plenty of similarities between the two operating systems. You will find that some DOS commands are virtually the same in UNIX; other DOS commands have UNIX counterparts, that, although they are named differently, are similar in function (see Table 3-1).

The commands that will be new to a DOS user provide capabilities that he or she has not found in DOS. In fact, most of the differences that do exist between the two environments result from the fact that UNIX is simply able to do much more.

Your UNIX Account

UNIX, being a multi-user system, is like a building that has offices assigned to individuals along with common areas that everyone uses. Each person has his or her own UNIX account.

To get into your account, you log in at your terminal and identify yourself. Usually, you have to enter your login name or ID and a password. The password does not appear on the screen as you type it.

Table 3-1. Comparison of DOS and UNIX Commands

DOS Command	UNIX Command
Concatenate Files	
COPY *file1* **+** *file2 file3*	**cat** *file1 file2 file3*
Copy all files to directory	
COPY *.* *dir*	**cp *** *dir*
Rename or relocate file	
REN *file1 file2*	**mv** *file1 file2*
Create new directory	
MKDIR *dir*	**mkdir** *dir*
Change directory	
CD \word	**cd /word**
List information about files	
DIR	**ls -l**
Delete file	
DEL *file*	**rm** *file*
Remove directory	
RMDIR *dir*	**rmdir** *dir*
Send file to screen	
TYPE *file*	
COPY CON FILE	**cat** *file*
Scroll file to screen	
TYPE *file* **| MORE**	**more (or pg)** *file*
Display current date and time	
DATE / TIME	**date**
Display lines matching string in file	
FIND *string file*	**grep** *string file*
Sort the contents of a file	
SORT *file*	**sort** *file*

```
System V Release 3.0 EXL 316

login:  fred
password:
```

Once you log in, you are in your home directory. It is your place on the file system, where you can create and store your own files.

The UNIX file system consists of many directories, some of which are dedicated to user accounts. Other directories contain programs and system files that are shared by all users.

The Shell

When you log on, the system initiates a sequence of actions to provide you with a computing environment. It starts a program called the *shell*, which will monitor all system interaction with you. This program displays a prompt on your terminal screen and waits for your input. The shell is equivalent to the DOS program *command.com.*

The standard System V shell is named the Bourne shell. Another popular shell (available on all Berkeley systems and some System V-derived systems) is known as the C shell (seashell). The system prompt for the Bourne shell is a dollar sign ($); the prompt for the C shell is a percent sign (%). We will use the Bourne shell in the examples shown throughout this chapter.

Who's On the System

On a multi-user system like UNIX, it is important to keep track of each individual who is logged in. Your login id is used to route mail to you and to control access to files you create.

The **who** command lists all users who are currently logged on to the system.

```
$ who

john     tty001        Oct 3 12:00
alice    tty004        Oct 3 09:00
```

The listing gives the user's login name, the name of the communications port (or tty device) that their terminal is attached to, and the date and time when they logged in.

Your User Profile

Each user has a personal copy of the shell; by modifying it, you can customize your computing environment.

When you boot a DOS system, the system looks for an *autoexec.bat* file and executes any commands it finds in there. Because DOS is a single-user system, the *autoexec.bat* file includes both system start up commands and those for customizing the user environment.

In UNIX, a similar process occurs each time you log in. The Bourne shell looks for and executes a file in your home directory called *profile*; the C shell uses two files called *.login* and *.cshrc*.

These files are normally invisible, since files whose name begins with a period will not show up in a directory listing unless you use the -a option with the **ls** command.

Usually, a generic version of *.profile* or *.login* and *.cshrc* is copied into your home directory by the system administrator. Feel free to modify the parts of it you understand. Typically, these files do three important things:

- Set the command search path to common system directories.
- Set your terminal type.
- Run any programs you want to have run automatically each time you log in. For example, many users invoke the **mail** program to read any electronic mail messages that may be waiting for them.

We'll discuss the **mail** program in a separate section.

OS, the shell allows users to define environment variables. The most im-rtant environment variable is PATH, which identifies the command search path. The concept is the same as in DOS (which is not surprising, since DOS derived this feature from UNIX). When you enter a command, the command processor looks in each of the directories listed in your search path. Typical UNIX command directories are */bin*, */usr/bin*, and */etc*. Other directories containing local commands are usually also specified by the administrator. Users can also set aside their own special command directories.

The following line sets a search path that includes the directories . (the current directory), */bin*, */usr/bin*, and */usr/tim/tools*.

```
PATH =.:/bin:/usr/bin:/usr/tim/tools;export PATH
```

The C shell uses a different syntax.

```
set path = (. /bin  /usr/bin /usr/tim/tools)
setenv path $path
```

Another important environment variable is TERM, which identifies what type of terminal you are using. There are a wide variety of terminal types, including ones that emulate an IBM-PC monitor and keyboard. (PC monitors display information on 25 lines, whereas most terminals use 24 lines.)

As long as information appears cleanly on your terminal screen, you probably don't have to worry about setting your terminal type. The administrator usually will set this up for you. However, if at your site, you support a wide variety of terminal types, and you log in at different terminals, you may need to set the terminal type yourself.

The following line sets the environment variable TERM to "vt100", a popular terminal type (developed by Digital Equipment Corporation and simulated by many terminal emulators).

```
$ TERM = vt100; export TERM
```

Or, in the C shell, you would type:

```
% setenv term vt100
```

UNIX has a database of terminal types that supports most popular terminals. If you encounter difficulties with your terminal, ask your system administrator or another person who uses the same type of terminal.

Using Electronic Mail

A major benefit of a multi-user system is the ability to communicate via electronic mail with other users. You can send or receive mail messages that you compose at your terminal. E-mail is an effective way of communicating ideas, information, and mindless chatter.

If the recipient is also logged in, the mail message that you send is delivered immediately. Otherwise, it is held in a "mail box" until that person does log in. After you read them, you can keep messages in your mail box, save them in a file, forward them to other users, or delete them.

Reading Your Mail

When you log into your system, or at any time when you are at prompt, you may see the following message:

```
$ You have mail.
```

This means someone has sent you mail. To read your mail, simply type **mail** at the system prompt.

```
$ mail
From Alice      Mon Oct 5    12:41
Can I have a printed copy of the Blake
memorandum that you sent me on line last week?

Thanks, Alice

?
```

Each mail message has a header that gives you the user id of the person that sent you the message and the date and time they sent it to you.

After the message appears, a question mark prompt is displayed. You can simply press Return to see the next message. When there are no more messages, you will exit the **mail** program and return to the system prompt.

There are also a number of commands that you enter at the mail prompt. For instance, if you just press Return, then the messages will remain in your mailbox. Usually, you want to use the **d** command to delete the message before quitting the program. You can use the **s** command followed by a filename to save the message in a file before deleting it.

Note: There are two mail programs available on System V, **mail** and **mailx**. **mail**, covered here, is simpler, but **mailx** has more features and is preferred by most advanced users. (On Berkeley UNIX systems, where it was developed, **mailx** is simply called **mail**.) The main differences are that **mailx** prompts you for a subject header when you send mail, and displays a message list summary when you invoke the program to read mail. Messages sent by one program can be received by the other.

UNIX Rules of Thumb

In this section, we discuss various conventions that are different in DOS and UNIX environments. These are presented as brief rules of thumb that should help you work more productively in UNIX.

File Naming Conventions

There are significant differences in DOS and UNIX file naming conventions. DOS file names typically have a maximum of eight characters, with an extension of exactly three characters.

UNIX filenames (in System V) can be up to fourteen characters in length. Filename extensions (i.e., *.wks* or *.txt*) are frequently not used, although some programs require them. (For example, files containing C source code always have the extension *.c*.)

Any legal filename on a DOS system will be legal on a UNIX system. However, the reverse is not true, so if you will be transferring files from one environment to the other, you might be well advised to stick to DOS naming conventions.

Case Sensitivity

Unlike DOS, UNIX is case-sensitive. Lower case and upper case letters are distinct. For instance, in UNIX, the following three filenames are unique; in DOS, they are not:

Nutshell
NUTSHELL
nutshell

By long-standing convention, all UNIX commands have lower-case names. However, both upper and lower case letters can be used in filenames.

Pathname Separators

In UNIX pathnames, directories and files are separated by a slash (/), not a backslash (\). For example:

```
$ cd /usr/john
```

Wildcards

Wildcards are special characters that are used to expand filenames. In UNIX, wildcards are often called metacharacters.

UNIX has the same wildcards as DOS, the asterisk (*) and question mark (?). There is a slight difference in the way that these wildcards are used in UNIX, however.

Because DOS makes use of filename extensions, a separate asterisk is required to represent both the filename and the extension. In DOS, *.* will match all files in the current directory. In UNIX, a single asterisk will have the same effect.

In both DOS and UNIX, the ? will match any single character in a file name. However, in DOS, it will match zero characters, while in UNIX, it must match at least one character. For example, assuming two files named *ch04* and *ch04a*, the file specification *ch04?* will match both files in DOS, while in UNIX it will match only *ch04a*.

In addition, in UNIX, brackets can be used to match one of several specified characters. [Mm]emo will match memo or Memo. A range of characters can be indicated by a hyphen. Thus, ch0[1-9] would match ch01, ch02, ch03, etc.

Command Line Options

Options modify the action of a command. For many commands, these options consist of a single letter, preceded by a minus sign (–). The letters that represent command line options are usually mnemonic. For instance, the **ls** command has a –C option for displaying the names of files in columns. (On Berkeley UNIX systems, **ls** does this automatically, without any option required.)

```
$ ls -C /usr/bin
awk        comm       find       lc         pg
banner     cp         getopt     line       prof
basename   cpio       glob       ls         ps
c          crypt      grep       mkdir      pwd
cal        egrep      head       mv         rev
cat        expr       help       nm         rm
cd         fg         jobs       nr         rmdir
chmod      fgrep      join       od         sed
cmp        file       kill       paste      vi
```

Spaces between commands, options, and filenames are important.

I/O Redirection and Pipes

When you enter a command at the keyboard, input is said to come from standard input; the result is directed to standard output, the user's display screen. Error messages are directed to standard error, which is also the terminal screen. Standard input, standard output, and standard error can be redirected from or to a file or another command.

The symbol > is used to redirect standard output to a file, overwriting its previous contents. The symbol >> can be used instead to append to the file. The symbol < is used to redirect standard input from a file.

Here are three command lines that demonstrate I/O redirection:

```
$ echo call home at 3:00 > reminders
$ echo pick up expense voucher >> reminders
$ mail tom < reminders
```

In addition, the output from one command can be sent as an input stream to another command. Just as in DOS, this is a *pipe* and is represented by the symbol (|). For example, to find out how many different commands are available on your UNIX system, you could type:

```
$ ls /bin /usr/bin | wc
229     227     1416
```

(Most common user commands are found in the directories */bin* and */usr/bin*. The **wc** program counts lines, words and characters, in that order, so the middle figure represents the number of commands in those two directories).

In general, you will find wider application of pipes and I/O redirection in UNIX than DOS because so many commands are stream-oriented. That is, most UNIX commands are designed to accept a stream of bytes as input, and produce a stream of bytes as output. Pipes and I/O redirection are fundamental to the design of most UNIX programs, instead of being an add-on, as they are in DOS.

Batch Command Files

In DOS, you can place commands in a **bat** file for execution. In UNIX, batch command files are called shell scripts. However, instead of using a filename extension to designate a command file, UNIX requires you to change the mode of the file—to make it executable. (We'll look at file modes later in this chapter.)

Let's say that we have placed the command in the previous section in a file named *howmany*. To make that file executable, we use the **chmod** command.

```
$ chmod +x howmany
```

Now, you can run the command by typing **howmany** at the system prompt. The output from the command will come to your screen. Unlike DOS, the commands themselves are not echoed on your screen. (We'll talk about **chmod** later in this chapter.)

Command line arguments can be passed into shell scripts using the notation ($1,$2,$3, etc.). The **howmany** shell script could be changed to specify the files from the command line:

```
ls $1 $2 | wc
```

The user would then be able to specify the names of one or two directories on the command line.

Shell scripts can be more complex than DOS **bat** files. The shell itself has a complete set of programming constructs for testing values, looping, prompting for input, and trapping error conditions. Many programmers use shell scripts to prototype procedures which they will later write in the C programming language.

For the user, shell scripts can be used to reduce repetitive procedures to a single command.

File Management

Table 3-1, which compares DOS and UNIX command equivalents, shows a list of the UNIX commands that you use to manage files. There are commands that allow you to view, concatenate, delete, move, or copy files. These functions are the same for any operating system, however different the individual commands that perform these functions may be.

UNIX has a hierarchical file system, just like most versions of DOS. Files are organized in directories and subdirectories. The top level directory is called the *root* directory.

Just as in DOS, you can move between directories using the **cd** command. The **pwd** command will display the name of the current directory.

When you specify a file, you can use its name, if the file is in the current directory. Otherwise, you have to supply its pathname. An absolute pathname is the path of directories that are descended from the root directory. A relative pathname is the path from the current directory.

Thus, if you were in the directory */usr/alice*, and wanted to access a file named notes in the directory */usr/fred*, you might use the absolute pathname:

```
$ pwd
/usr/alice
$ ls -l /usr/fred/notes
```

If you were in the directory */usr*, and wanted to access */usr/fred/notes*, you could enter a relative pathname:

```
$ pwd
/usr
$ ls fred/notes
```

Directory Listings

In DOS, you use the **dir** command to obtain a listing of files in a directory. In UNIX, the equivalent is the **ls** command.

If you were running Merge/386 or VP/ix, you could use either the DOS or UNIX command (**dir** or **ls**) to get a directory listing. However, each command gives you a different amount of information.

The **ls** command without any options will list the files in the current directory. Unlike DOS, UNIX sorts the filenames alphabetically. If you want to list the files in columns, use the **–C** option. The **–l** option presents a *long* listing that tells you the size of the file, its owner and group, size, and time and date of creation or last modification.

```
$ ls -l

total 53
ch00    -rw-r--r-- 1 fred  doc  1003 Sep 29 16:31
ch01    -rw-r--r-- 1 fred  doc  2625 Sep 29 16:17
ch01    -rw-r--r-- 1 fred  doc  3951 Sep 29 21:13
ch02    -rw-r--r-- 1 fred  doc  4966 Sep 29 21:47
ch03    -rw-r----- 1 fred  doc  1396 Sep 29 16:04
chips   -rw-rw-rw- 1 alex  mkt  1200 Sep 28 23:28
vp      drwxrwxrwx 1 fred  doc     0 Sep 24 15:06
vp.old  -rwxrwxrwx 1 john  sys    80 Sep 24 15:22
```

File Permissions

When you have a group of users sharing the same system, it is important to offer some method of restricting access to different parts of the system.

File security in UNIX is accomplished by setting file permission modes. The owner of a file can specify who can read (r), write (w) or execute (x) a file. An executable file is either a compiled program, or, as shown earlier, a file that contains a shell script. These permissions can be set separately for owner, group and all others. (When the administrator sets up an account for you, he or she assigns you a login id and a group id. For example, all the people in market research might be assigned to the same group, *msearch.*)

The file *ch03* in the listing in the previous example shows read and write permissions for the file's owner *fred*, read permissions for members of the group *doc*, and no permissions for other users. This means that only the owner could modify the contents of this file. Members of the group could read or make copies of the file. No others could access it.

The **chmod** command can be used to change the permissions for a file, providing that you are the owner of the file. The following command sets write permissions for all three classes of users:

```
$ chmod +w ch01
```

Now, any user can modify the file *ch01*. The option **–w** removes write permissions for all sets. Similarly, +/**–r** and +/**–x** add or remove read and execute privileges, respectively. To apply the command only to a specific class of users, prefix the permission assignment with the character **u** for user (yourself), **g** for group, or **o** for other. Permission assignments can be combined into a single command. For example, the following command will remove read and write permission from anyone but the file's owner:

```
$ chmod go-rw ch01
```

In the case of directories, permissions work slightly differently than they do for plain files. For a directory, execute permission means the permission to search the directory—for example, to do an **ls** listing on it. Therefore, to restrict access to an entire directory, you can simply remove execute permission for a particular class of users.

UNIX has always tended to be an open system. By default, your files will probably be read/write by all users. If you want to set a different default for all files you create, you can do so by issuing the **umask** command in your *.profile* or *.login* file. **umask** specifies permissions by means of an octal value. While it is a little awkward to use, you don't need it very frequently, and the most typical values are easily ascertainable from the documentation.

See the UNIX documentation on **chmod** and **umask** for more details.

Print Spooling

With a PC, you probably had a dedicated printer. It was connected to your machine and only you could use it. You could send it only one print job at a time and had to wait until the printing finished before you could resume work.

UNIX uses a print spooler to allow many users to share a single printer. A user can make a printing request at any time, even if the printer is currently busy. Requests are queued and processed in order as the printer becomes available.

If you haven't worked on a system that employs a spooler, you may have to remind yourself to be patient. Remember, there are other printing jobs that may be in the queue before yours. This drawback is easily offset by the benefit that you don't need to wait for printing to finish before you can get back to work.

UNIX permits multiple printers to be connected to the same system. If there is more than one printer, one printer is set up as the default printer and print jobs are automatically sent there.

In System V, the **lp** command is used to queue a print job. (Berkeley systems use a different set of printer commands than are shown here, but the functions are analogous.) When you use **lp**, it spools the file for printing and returns the request id of your print job. The request id can later be used to cancel the print job, if you decide to do so.

```
$ lp notes
request-id is lp-2354 (1 file)
```

The **lpstat** command can be used to check on the status of your print jobs.

The **lpstat** command will tell whether your job is in the queue.

```
$ lpstat
lp-2354                    14519 fred  on lp
```

The message *on lp* indicates that the job is currently printing. If your job does not appear at all on the listing, it means your job has finished printing.

If the job is listed, but the *on lp* message does not appear, then the job is still in the queue. You can see the status of all jobs in the queue with the **–u** option. You can cancel a job with the **cancel** command.

```
$ lpstat -u
lp-2354                 14519 fred  on lp
lp-2355                 21321 alice
lp-2356                  9065 john
$ cancel lp-2356
lp-2356:  cancelled
```

The **lpstat** command can be used to determine what printers are connected to your system and their names. If there is more than one printer, you can then use the **–d** option with **lp** to specify a printer destination other than the default. For instance, if a laser printer is configured as *laserp*, then you can enter:

```
$ lp -dlaserp myfile
```

to print *myfile* on printer **laserp**.

Editors

One of the most useful tools in the UNIX environment is the full screen text editor **vi**. One of the glaring deficiencies of the DOS environment is its lack of a good text editor. On the other hand, many DOS users know how to use a word processing program to create and edit ASCII text files. An editor is a general purpose program which can be used to create mail messages, letters, shell scripts, and computer programs.

You can learn a subset of editing commands fairly quickly and become productive. The **vi** editor has two modes: *command* mode and *insert* mode. You are in command mode when you begin. Then you give a single-letter command (like **a** or **i**) to enter insert mode. While in insert mode, you can type away just like at a typewriter keyboard. To quit insert mode, you press the ESC key.

If you have used Microsoft Word on the PC, you are probably used to switching between command mode and insert mode already. In fact, Microsoft Word also uses the ESC key to switch modes.

Another benefit of learning a UNIX editor is that you will learn about regular expressions, a powerful pattern-matching facility used in a number of UNIX commands, such as **grep, awk**, and **sed.**

grep is more or less equivalent to the DOS **find** command—it locates a text string in a file or in a stream of data passed to it through a pipe.

sed and **awk** are powerful editors with no equivalents in DOS. They allow you to write editing scripts to modify files from the outside, or even to modify data in a pipe.

For a complete introduction to the **vi** editor, see the Nutshell Handbook *Learning the vi Editor*. For more information on **sed** and **awk**, see the Nutshell Handbook, *Advanced Editing Tools.*

Multi-tasking

Multi-tasking, a significant capability of UNIX not found in DOS, allows users to run more than one program at once. In DOS, when you enter a command, you have to wait for it to finish before the command prompt returns to your screen. In UNIX, you can put a slow or long-running program in the *background*, freeing up your terminal for other work.

The "&" character is placed at the end of a command line to specify that a program be executed in the background. For instance, if you were going to run the **grep** program to locate every occurrence of the string UNIX in a hundred text files, you could process the command in the background, and redirect the output to a file called *justunix*.

```
$ grep "UNIX" manual/* > justunix &
[1] 9870
$
```

When you put a command in the background, UNIX gives you its process ID; in this case, it is 9870. The **ps** command can be used to list all of your processes and will tell you if background job is still running.

```
$ ps
  PID      TTY   TIME       COMMAND
 6569      006   0:12       sh
 9870      006   1:23       grep
 9888      006   0:02       ps
```

This listing tells you the process ID (PID), your terminal or port number (TTY), the amount of CPU time that the process has used so far, and the name of the command. The above list contains the your login shell process, the **grep** background process, and the **ps** process that you have just invoked.

Generally, you don't need to worry about your background process. A message will appear on your screen informing you that the process has completed. However, you may want to "kill" a background process before it finishes, especially if you suspect that something may be wrong. The **kill** command can be used to kill any background process that you initiated. You need to know the process ID to kill it, however.

```
$ kill 9870
[1] Terminated    grep
```

If you need to kill a chain of commands, you can specify multiple process IDs in a single kill command.

On Berkeley UNIX systems, the C shell supports a much more powerful method of handling background processes, called *job control.* Job control allows you to suspend a process that is already running in the foreground (perhaps to put it in the background), or to bring a background job to the foreground, as well as to kill a background job.

Some recent System V implementations include a mechanism called "shell layers" which has something of the same effect. And on the many UNIX workstations with windowing systems, you can of course have multiple login sessions going on at the same time, each one in a separate window.

In Conclusion

This chapter gave you an idea of what it would be like to move from a DOS environment to a UNIX environment. For a look at some of the specific features of the software products that integrate the two environments, see Chapters 4 through 7.

4

PC-Interface: The PC in a Larger Context

This chapter introduces you to the workings of PC-Interface and gives you a closer look at some of the features described in Chapter 2. Since PC-NFS is a very similar product (based on the same code), this chapter discusses PC-Interface only.

PC-Interface provides the DOS user with three functional modes:

- Host File Services lets you use a UNIX system as a file and print server.
- Remote Command Execution lets you use stream-oriented UNIX commands on DOS files.
- Terminal Emulation lets you log in to a UNIX host and use your PC as a terminal.

Remember that PC-Interface is most appropriate for connecting a standalone PC to a UNIX host. The PC may be connected with either an Ethernet or an RS-232 connection, and the UNIX modules for PC-Interface must already be installed on the host. If Ethernet is used, the PC can optionally be connected to more than one host (though not simultaneously.) The PC can have as little as 128K of memory, and only one floppy disk drive.

For the sake of demonstration, let's say that we are working at a PC with a fixed disk (Drive C:) on which the PC-Interface software is loaded, and that the PC is connected to the UNIX host via an Ethernet. PC-Interface establishes the UNIX file system as a virtual drive in DOS (Drive D:). If the PC did not have a fixed disk of its own, PC-Interface would mount the UNIX file system as virtual drive C:. If drive D: were already in use on the PC, the UNIX file system would be drive E:. See Figure 4-1.

Host File Services

Host File Services mode allows a DOS user to use the UNIX system as a file and print server.

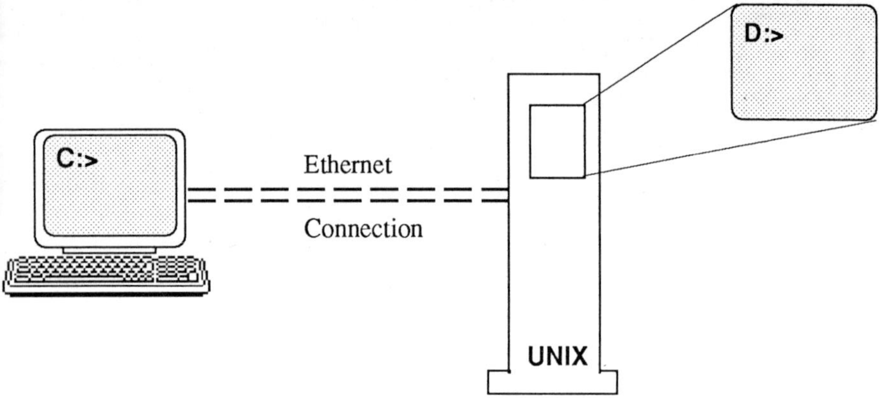

Figure 4-1
The UNIX disk appears to the PC as if it were its own Drive D:.

To use PC-Interface's host file services, you must have a login account on the UNIX system, although you need not ever actually interact directly with UNIX after you have supplied your user name and password.

To enter Host File Services mode, you enter the PC-Interface **login** command at the DOS C> prompt. PC-Interface will display a menu of available UNIX hosts. Once you have selected a host, PC-Interface will make the connection to the UNIX system, and you will be prompted for your login name and password, just as if you were logging on from a terminal. However, once you have logged on successfully, instead of the UNIX shell prompt, the following message appears on the PC screen:

```
Welcome to PC-Interface
Unix File System Available as Drive D:
C>
```

To close the connection with the UNIX host, simply type the **logout** command at the DOS prompt.

Working With the Virtual Drive

In Host File Services mode, files residing on the remote UNIX host can be accessed as though they were on a local fixed disk.

You can copy a file to or from the virtual drive just as you would copy it to or from a floppy in the A: drive. For that matter, you can copy programs to the virtual disk and run them from there.

The following command copies the file *notes* from the virtual drive (D:) to the directory *word* on the PC hard disk.

```
C> copy D:notes C:\word
```

The next command copies the file *sample.doc* from the PC's hard disk to the virtual drive in the UNIX file system:

```
C> copy sample.doc D:
```

You can also access this file for a local application, such as Microsoft Word:

```
C> word D:sample.doc
```

You can make the virtual drive your default drive:

```
C> D:
D>
```

You can even copy an application such as Microsoft Word to the virtual drive, and use it to edit files on either the virtual drive or on an actual PC drive:

```
D> copy C:\word.exe
word.exe          1 File(s) copied
D> word c:autoexec.bat
```

The D: drive corresponds to your home directory in the UNIX file system. If you enter **dir D:**, you will get a DOS-style directory listing of the files in your UNIX home directory. However, this directory is the *root* directory for the virtual drive. Thus, the UNIX pathname of the file *sample.doc* in John's home directory might actually be */usr/john/sample.doc*.

Note: In DOS, a backslash separates the parts of a pathname; in UNIX, a slash is used.

There are several non-obvious implications to this correspondence. Files on the virtual drive will appear to users on the UNIX system simply as files in your home directory. Depending on file access permissions (see Chapter 3), these files can be accessed by other UNIX users, or even moved to other directories in the UNIX file system. However, the DOS user will only be able to access files that are stored in his or her UNIX home directory, since he or she doesn't have a view of the rest of the UNIX file system.

Each PC user can have his or her own personal D: drive on the UNIX file system. If several PC-Interface users want to share the same virtual drive on the UNIX system, they will need to be given login accounts with the same home directory. Obviously, it would be easy enough to assign personal subdirectories within the DOS environment.

There are also a few complications caused by differences between UNIX and DOS in:

- File naming conventions
- File formats
- File access permissions

File Naming Conventions

A minor difference between UNIX and DOS is their file naming conventions. Although all DOS file names are valid under UNIX, the reverse is not necessarily true. UNIX filenames can contain up to fourteen characters (even more on Berkeley UNIX systems), and are not limited to a three character extension following a period. For example, a perfectly reasonable UNIX file name might be *chapter.seven*.

Rather than simply truncating any UNIX filename that is invalid under DOS, PC-Interface automatically maps it to a legal DOS name. While the mapped DOS filename is shorter and less readable, it does allow the UNIX file to be accessed by DOS applications.

Because filename mapping is done automatically, you do not have to worry about the filenaming conflicts of the two environments. It might only affect you if you are accessing files created by UNIX users or by yourself during a UNIX login session. To make it easy on yourself, as a rule, observe the DOS filenaming conventions even while in UNIX.

If your UNIX home directory already contains a number of files with names that flout DOS conventions, you may prefer to rename the files, or to use the PC-Interface **udir** command instead of **dir** to list your files.

If you use the standard DOS **dir** command, its listing will contain the mapped name of any non-conforming UNIX files. For example:

```
D> dir
 Volume in drive D is EXL-316
 Directory of D:\
.             <DIR>          12-14-87    8:45a
..            <DIR>          11-21-87    4:31p
CH01     TXT         13441   12-21-87    8:12p
STATU{KRE}           24642   12-16-87    7:23a
        4 File(s)       2341258 bytes free
```

The UNIX filename *statusreport* was truncated, and a unique index applied to create the rather obscure mapped name *STATU{KRE}*.

The PC-Interface **udir** command combines the standard DIR listing with a list in the manner of the UNIX command **ls -l**, displaying the original UNIX filename beside the mapped filename.

```
D> udir
 Volume in drive D is EXL-316
 Directory of D:\
.            .           tim drwxr-xr-x <DIR> 12-14-87 8:45a
..           ..          tim drwxr-xr-x <DIR> 11-21-87 4:31p
ch01.txt     CH01 TXT    tim -rw-r--r-- 13441 12-21-87 8:12p
statusreport STATU{KRE} tim -rw-r--r-- 24642 12-16-87 7:23a
          4 File(s)        2341258 bytes free
```

This command gives you the perspective of both environments on a single directory.

You could rename the file *statusreport* either by using the mapped name with the DOS **rename** command:

```
D> ren statu{kre} status.rpt
```

or by using the PC-Interface command **uren**, which allows you to rename a file using either a source or destination name that does not correspond to DOS conventions:

```
D> uren statusreport status.rpt
```

As we'll see later, you could also use PC-Interface's ON utilities to invoke the UNIX **mv** command to rename the file.

File Formats

Another area for conflict between the two environments is that the format of DOS and UNIX text files are slightly different. UNIX text files have a linefeed (LF) at the end of each line; DOS files have a carriage return and a linefeed (CR/LF). In addition, DOS text files use ^Z as an end of file marker. Depending upon the application, users may need to translate UNIX and DOS text files explicitly. Two commands are provided: **dos2unix** and **unix2dos**. For example, you might use the **dos2unix** command if you wanted to use the **vi** editor on a DOS file.

When executing remote commands using PC-Interface's ON utilities (these utilities bring many powerful UNIX tools to the DOS user), the translation of text files is performed automatically.

File Access Permissions

As a multi-user system, UNIX has security mechanisms that are foreign to DOS. As described in Chapter 3, file access permissions control which users can read, modify, or execute files, or search directories.

As a DOS user accessing the UNIX file system only through PC-Interface's virtual disk, you may never need to concern yourself with UNIX file permissions. However, if you do decide to avail yourself of this mechanism, in order to protect your files from reading or modification by other users, you can do so. PC-Interface includes a command called **uchmod**, which works similarly to the UNIX **chmod** command described in Chapter 3, but which can be run from DOS.

Because of the way certain DOS programs work, however, permissions may not give you the expected level of protection. For example, if you use a program like WordStar to modify a file, it actually renames the file (a legitimate operation even with UNIX's read-only permissions) with a .BAK extension, and then replaces it with a new file. As a result, to truly protect the file from other users, you may need to deny even read permission. This is an area where you may need to experiment on a case by case basis.

Print Service

While in File Services mode, you can use a local printer connected to the personal computer or a remote printer connected to a UNIX system. You can establish either the local or the remote printer as the default printer for his or her working session.

Using a local printer is done as it is normally done in DOS, directing output to one of the LPT channels. A remote printer is logically mapped to a DOS communications port as iollows:

```
C> printer LPT1 remote "lp -dlaser"
```

Requests sent to LPT1 are now directed to the UNIX system where the print command **lp -dlaser** is executed. In this case, the UNIX print command uses the **lp** spooler to send a request to the destination *laser*, a laser printer. The logical mapping of a remote print command to a DOS printer port means that the remote printer can be accessed from within DOS applications without any special setup.

You can specify a different UNIX print command to correspond to each logical printer DOS supports. Or you can assign them to a standard DOS printer. So, for example, you could assign LPT1 to a locally attached dot-matrix printer, LPT2 to a laser printer on the UNIX system, and LPT3 to a high speed line printer on the UNIX system.

Remote Command Execution

From Host File Services mode, a PC user can execute commands on the remote UNIX system. The implementation of this feature is so transparent, however, that the user thinks he or she has simply expanded the utilities available in the DOS environment.

PC-Interface provides optional ON utilities that allow a DOS user to run the (non-interactive) stream-oriented commands of the UNIX environment on DOS files. The output from a command can then be redirected to other DOS or UNIX commands. The ON utilities provide an alternative to terminal emulation, since you don't have to log on to the UNIX host system to execute UNIX commands.

For instance, if you wanted to use UNIX's powerful pattern matching command **grep** to locate occurences of a string in a DOS file, you could type:

```
C> on grep "^123" dosfile
```

Any UNIX utility or shell script can be executed in this way. Additionally, you can set up your DOS environment so that you can access UNIX commands without entering **on**. Let's take for example the UNIX *spell* program. All that needs to be done to make that command available in the DOS environment is to copy the PC-Interface program *on.exe* to *spell.exe* (making sure that the new command is in a directory in your search path). Then you can enter that command just as you would in UNIX:

```
C>  spell dosfile
```

The DOS **copy** command makes a physical duplicate of the *on.exe* file. The copy can reside in a DOS directory or in a UNIX directory on the virtual drive.

There is one big advantage to storing ON utilities on the virtual drive. In UNIX, you can link different names to the same file. A link is a pointer to the original file, rather than an actual duplicate copy. Links can save disk space and work just as effectively.

The very first time you create a link, you will want to link *on.exe* to *ln.exe* on the virtual drive. First copy *on.exe* from its location on the PC floppy or fixed disk to the virtual disk. Then make the link.

```
D> copy a:on.exe
on.exe     1 File(s) copied
D> on ln on.exe ln.exe
```

Then you can use the new **ln** command to create links to other commands.

```
D>  ln on.exe spell.exe
```

If you are going to create links to *on.exe* on the virtual disk, you should be sure to add the appropriate directory to your DOS search path. For example, if you created a subdirectory called *commands* on the virtual disk, the PATH command in your *autoexec.bat* file might look like this:

```
PATH C:\;C\DOS;C:\BAT;D:\COMMANDS
```

This is also true if you copy any DOS programs to the virtual disk.

(If you copy DOS programs to the virtual disk, you should be aware of any restrictions that the programs themselves enforce on the search path. For example, WordStar requires that files to be edited be found in the same directory as the program itself. Likewise, if a copy-protected program requires you to insert a key disk in drive A:, you will still need to do so. Of course, you face exactly these same restrictions if you copy the program to a local fixed disk on the DOS system.)

PC-Interface's ON utilities cannot be used to access interactive UNIX programs. The **vi** editor and **mail**, or any specialized screen-oriented application, must be run from Terminal Emulation mode, as described later in this chapter.

However, most standard UNIX programs are stream-oriented, that is, they operate on and produce a character stream that can be redirected to a file or piped to another command. PC-Interface allows you to use the pipe and redirection facilities of DOS or UNIX to create a command stream from one environment to the other. In fact, you can send mail using the ON utilities because input can be redirected from a file; but you cannot read mail because the **mail** program prompts you for input.

Terminal Emulation

Terminal Emulation mode allows you to use your PC like a terminal and log in to an account on the UNIX system. This mode is similar to the terminal emulation programs described in Chapter 2. PC-Interface lets you switch back and forth between Host File Services mode and Terminal Emulation mode. For example, you could be logged on to one UNIX host in Terminal Emulation mode and alternate that session with a Host File Services mode session on a second UNIX host.

In a departmental computing environment, Terminal Emulation mode can be used in various ways. It can give PC users access to UNIX applications or it can transform an unused but available PC into a UNIX terminal.

If you are working in Host File Services mode, and wish to begin a UNIX user session, enter the **em** command at a DOS prompt. (If you are not in Host File Services mode to begin with, you will have to identify the UNIX host before beginning your session.) Once you are logged in, you will see a UNIX prompt and you can enter any UNIX command. See Chapter 3 for a discussion of working in the UNIX environment.

Other DOS-UNIX Networking Products

PC-Interface is not the only product that allows PCs and UNIX systems to share files. XenixNet, available from the Santa Cruz Operation or other resellers of Xenix (Microsoft's version of UNIX), allows Xenix systems to share files with other Xenix systems or with DOS systems running IBM's PC network software. Each machine on the network is given a unique node name. Users on other machines can refer to files on each others' disk by an extended pathname syntax of the form: *//nodename/pathname.*

The Xenix/PC Network combination does PC-Interface one better in that it allows Xenix users to access files on a DOS disk. However, DOS users are not able to run UNIX programs on their files.

ViaNet, from Western Digital Corp., is paired with Interactive's VP/ix against the PC-Interface/Merge combination available from Locus. ViaNet is very similar to PC-Interface. However, like XenixNet, and unlike PC-Interface, it allows UNIX users to access a DOS machine's disk.

ViaNet takes yet another approach to file sharing. To a DOS user, each node on the network appears to be a directory on a Z: drive. Disk drives on that node appear as directories. For example, the file *C:\123files\budget.wk1* on the machine *dosnode1* might be accessed from UNIX by the pathname:

Z:/dosnode1/C:/123files/budget.wk1.

The file */usr/tim/ch01.txt* on node *unix1* could be accessed by the pathname:

Z:=\unix1\usr\tim\ch01.txt.

ViaNet does not allow a DOS user to run UNIX utilities, but includes simulations of many common UNIX commands. Both XenixNet and ViaNet also provide terminal emulators, so DOS users can log in directly to UNIX.

```
System V Release 3.0 EXL 316
demosys
Copyright (C) 1986 AT&T
All Rights Reserved.

$
```

In Terminal Emulation mode, your terminal emulates a VT100, a popular terminal designed by Digital Equipment Corp. The VT100 emulation does not support all the special keys on your PC, so you cannot expect them to work the way they do in DOS. For instance, pressing the ALT key will have no effect.

During a terminal emulation session, you can return to Host File Services mode, and continue working in the DOS environment. Press F10 (function key 10) to return to DOS. This does not end your terminal emulation session, though, and you can return to your UNIX session from DOS by entering the **em** command again.

If you want to quit Terminal Emulation mode and not return to UNIX, you type **logout** to end your UNIX session. Then press F7 (function key 7) to close Terminal Emulation mode. Pressing F10 then returns you to the DOS prompt.

If your PC is physically connected to the UNIX host that acts as a file server on your network, it is most appropriate to use Host File Services mode. If your PC is connected to some other UNIX host, then you'd use the file transfer capabilities in Terminal Emulation mode.

PC-Interface's terminal emulator provides fairly rudimentary facilities for transferring files between DOS and UNIX. Text files can be "uploaded" by redirecting output on the UNIX system to a file, then selecting a command from a PC-Interface menu to send the DOS files. For the most part, you should use host file services to transfer files between DOS and UNIX.

5
DOS Under UNIX: Hardware Issues

PC-Interface lets a DOS-based PC use a UNIX system as a file and print server, and lets the UNIX file system masquerade as a "virtual disk" on the PC. It also lets you run UNIX utilities on your PC. However, with PC-Interface, the user is still sitting at the same familiar PC keyboard and display.

Merge and VP/ix go much further: they create an entire "virtual PC," making it possible to run DOS applications without having a PC at all. This introduces a whole new level of complication. While some users may be able to use DOS from the system console or compatible display terminals, others may want to run DOS applications from the standard ASCII terminals available with most UNIX systems.

In this chapter, we'll look at some of the hardware issues involved in using DOS on a UNIX system rather than on a PC. In later chapters, we'll try to give you a feel for what it's like to actually use these products.

DOS and the Intel Processors

The original IBM PC used an Intel 8088 processor. Later PC compatibles switched to the slightly more powerful Intel 8086. The PC-AT and compatibles used Intel's next-generation processor, the 80286. The latest crop of PCs—IBM's PS/2 family and competing systems from Compaq and others—use the vastly more powerful Intel 80386 processor.

A major difference between these successive generations of processor (apart from raw computational speed) is the size of the data they can process at one time, and the amount of memory they can address.

The 8088 and 8086 are both 16-bit processors. This means that at any one time, they can manipulate a binary number containing 16-bits. However, the 8088 has only an 8-bit data path, meaning that it takes two operations to load the processor with a full 16 bits of data, or to write that data back out to memory.

The number of bits the processor can handle at one time also determines the number of unique locations (or addresses) it can keep track of—essentially, how high it can count. This number is sometimes referred to as the processor's "address space."

By all rights, the 8088 and 8086 should have an address space of only 64K (2^{16}). However, these chips use a special "segment register" to increase the address width to 20 bits. This allows them to use a full megabyte of memory. Part of this address space is used to address devices other than memory, leading to the famous "640K memory barrier" enforced by DOS on all applications.

The 80286 and 80386 are both 32-bit processors; but like the 8088, the 80286 is only half-there—it has a 16-bit data path. However, both the 80286 and 80386 can address a full 32 bits (4 gigabytes or 2^{32}) of memory.

Unfortunately, DOS itself is still stuck with the 640K memory limitation imposed by the original 8088/8086 processors. There have been a number of extended memory schemes that allow DOS to address more memory, but most programs are unable to take advantage of the newer processor's greater power. IBM and Microsoft have introduced OS/2 because DOS is simply not able to keep up with the advanced hardware of the 80386.

The 80386 goes even further than the 80286 in that it supports a memory addressing technique called "virtual memory." Virtual memory divorces programs from the amount of a machine's physical memory. Instead of reading from and writing to actual memory locations, programs read and write locations in an arbitrary (or "virtual") memory space. Special memory-mapping hardware in the processor translates these virtual memory addresses to real addresses, keeping most-frequently used data in physical memory and swapping other data out to disk if necessary. "Privilege" mechanisms are used to separate the code that manages the overall operation of the system from the code that makes up user applications.

While not absolutely essential, virtual memory is very important for a high-performance multi-user, multi-tasking system. Note that even though the Intel 80386 processor supports virtual memory, DOS can't make use of this capability. UNIX can. As we'll see later in this chapter, DOS programs run in a special mode in which the 80386 emulates an 8086.

Processors Used with UNIX

Unlike DOS, which runs only on Intel processors, UNIX was designed to be portable, and has been re-engineered or "ported" to just about every advanced processor available today.

UNIX was originally developed on Digital Equipment Corp's PDP-7 processor, popularized on the Digital PDP-11, and then migrated to Digital's high-end VAX family of processors. Today, UNIX runs on many proprietary systems, including mainframes and supercomputers as well as microprocessors.

However, UNIX really took off when it was ported to the Motorola 68000 family of processors. The Motorola processors have been used as the basis of UNIX systems from many different manufacturers. These processors all use 32-bit addresses; the 68010, 68020, and the new 68030 support virtual memory.

Versions of UNIX are also available for all of the Intel processors, although the 80386 is the first with enough power to give UNIX full scope for its capabilities. Especially with products like Merge and VP/ix, which use large amounts of memory, virtual memory makes the difference between smooth functioning and a crashing halt to multi-user operation.

While DOS has been unable to make the transition to more powerful processors, UNIX has consistently grown with the hardware, and looks to be an ideal platform for future systems.

The 80386 is attracting particular attention from UNIX system manufacturers right now because it offers the possibility of running both DOS and UNIX on the same machine.

How Merge and VP/ix Work

Merge and VP/ix use the capabilities of the Intel 80286 and 80386 chips to create a "virtual machine" for PC applications.

These chips have a number of special modes designed to ensure backwards compatibility with previous Intel processors. It is because of this backward compatibility that you can take the same copy of Lotus 1-2-3 that you bought for your original IBM PC, and run it on your new Compaq 386. Unfortunately, when you do this, you fail to take advantage of the real power of the more advanced processor. You gain increased speed, but are otherwise limited to the capabilities of the original 8086 chip. Programs run in "real mode," which more or less means that they treat the 80386 as if it were "really" an 8086.

The UNIX operating system, by contrast, is able to use the processor's native 32-bit protected mode. This mode allows the use of virtual memory and provides privilege mechanisms that make true multi-tasking operation possible.

Under Merge 386 and VP/ix, programs originally designed for the 8086 microprocessor—including MS-DOS itself—run on the 386 in a special mode called virtual-8086 mode.

The virtual-8086 mode was designed specifically to allow DOS programs (which typically have been designed to act as though they own the entire machine, often directly manipulating screen memory or device control registers rather than going through the operating system's Basic Input/Output System, or BIOS) to run under a multi-tasking, virtual memory system such as UNIX.

All of the PC's normal memory addresses are mapped to virtual addresses, allowing a DOS program to act just as it always did, without any danger of it interfering with other programs or the operating system as a whole. In fact, multiple instances of DOS are able to run at the same time, each one under the illusion that it owns the entire machine. The emulation is so complete that it is even possible to "reboot" the virtual machine using DOS's CTRL-ALT-DEL key combination.

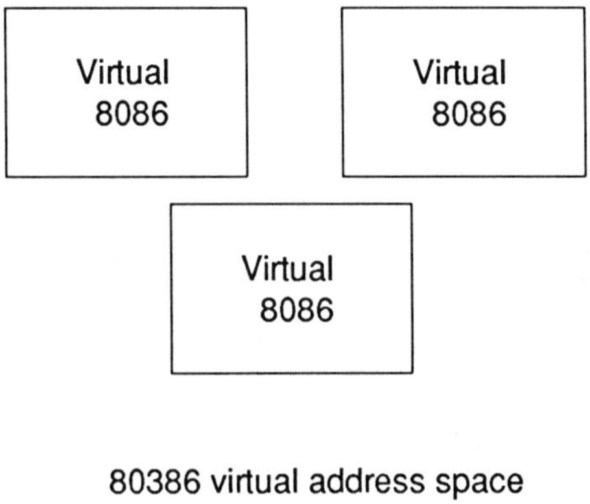

Figure 5-1
Multiple virtual 8086's can exist in the 80386's virtual address space.

The 286 processor has more limited support for DOS under UNIX. The 286 lacks a virtual-8086 mode. Under Merge 286, UNIX runs in the 286 processor's 16-bit protected mode, but DOS programs must still run in real mode. Merge 286 acts as a traffic cop, switching the system back and forth between the two modes. One implication is that only one instance of DOS can be run at a time. Furthermore, an ill-behaved DOS program can crash the entire system.

You should be aware therefore that even though Merge is available for both the 286 and 386 processors, the 386 version is far more robust and powerful. VP/ix is available only for the 386.

For more information on the differences between the 286 and 386 processors, and the mechanisms used to support DOS under UNIX, see Appendix A.

A Virtual 8086 Does Not Quite a PC Make

While the virtual 8086 mode of the 80386 processor makes it possible to run the DOS operating system and most DOS applications, there are other hardware issues that may place limits on your use of DOS under UNIX.

Most significant are differences between the display and keyboard of a PC console and those of the ASCII terminals used on most UNIX systems.

Display Types

As discussed earlier in this chapter, the typical ASCII terminal used on a UNIX system is character-based. A program sends out ASCII codes (including escape sequences for cursor placement or special effects such as highlighting or underscores). These codes are interpreted by a "character generator" in the terminal, which knows how to print the specified characters.

By contrast, the standard PC console has a *memory-mapped* graphic display. That is, programs draw on the display by writing to a reserved area of memory which is then *mapped* onto the display.

Fortunately, almost all DOS programs support the low-end display adaptor that has always been available for PCs, namely the MDA (Monochrome Display Adaptor), which is character-based, just like an ASCII terminal. As a result, it is possible for Merge and VP/ix to run most DOS programs (including such standards as 1-2-3) on an ASCII terminal just by emulating the MDA.

Are Multi-User DOS Applications Legal?

Manufacturers and resellers of products such as Merge and VP/ix are quiet on the subject. The fact is, though, that the ability to run an application such as 1-2-3 on a multi-user system raises legal questions. The shrink-wrap agreement on many microcomputer software products limits their use to a single CPU.

If this is the case, multi-user access is within the letter, though perhaps not the spirit, of the original agreement. In a bulletin entitled *SCO VP/ix: Technical Questions and Answers*, the Santa Cruz Operation advises, "Customers should read the license for each application they intend to run under VP/ix, and if in doubt consult with the company who licenses that application."

This is clearly a case where technology has outraced law. For many users eager to run DOS applications under UNIX, it may also be a case where, as Shakespeare said, "the hot blood leaps over the cold decree." Only time will tell how the lawyers for application developers will respond to this newest technological challenge.

However, MDA emulation doesn't solve every problem, even for character-based applications. The PC display has 25 lines, while the typical ASCII terminal has only 24. In order to solve this problem, both Merge and VP/ix define a special "rocker key" that lets you scroll the display on an ASCII terminal up or down one line so that you can see the full display (though not all at once).

A further problem is that even on an MDA, the PC character set includes a number of special graphics characters that are not part of standard ASCII. Most ASCII terminals cannot display these characters. Merge displays them as an asterisk; VP/ix lets you define your own equivalents in a terminal description file. This is an adequate solution.

In addition, in the past couple of years, a new type of terminal, called a PC-scancode terminal, has come on to the market. These terminals fully emulate the MDA display. They include the full 25 lines required of a PC display, and support the IBM extended graphics character set. As we'll see in the next section, they also have a standard IBM keyboard, which is at least as important.

Examples of this type of terminal include the Wyse WY-60 and the Televideo PCS1. At this point, though, nearly every major terminal vendor offers at least one scancode terminal. Scancode terminals provide a satisfactory solution for running character-based applications. However, graphics programs such as Microsoft Flight Simulator can only be run on a memory-mapped display.

Memory-mapped displays require a much larger amount of data to be transferred than would be possible with a serial link. (For example, in its high-resolution monochrome mode, an IBM CGA has a resolution of 640 x 200, or a total of 128,000 pixels. At 9600 bits per second, it would take more than 13 seconds to paint the screen.)

In order to achieve high data transfer rates, the PC console must be connected directly to the processor and memory by a high speed bus. Remote terminals running graphics applications have not been a possibility—at least until recently. Sun River's recently introduced bit-mapped terminal has been specifically designed to run DOS graphics applications on a multi-user machine. It is connected to the system with a high-speed fiber-optic link rather than an RS-232 cable.

Most 386-based machines have at least one PC-style console display, which will allow you to run DOS graphics programs under Merge or VP/ix. Depending on the machine, it may be possible to add additional memory-mapped terminals by using special graphics boards. With the Sun River fiber optic station mentioned earlier in this chapter, you can have as many memory-mapped terminals as you can afford!

Keyboard Mapping

In addition to having different display requirements, many DOS programs also rely on special keys on the PC keyboard that are not available on standard ASCII terminals. These keys include ALT, PrtSc, PgUp and PgDn. In addition, some terminals lack function keys or even cursor movement keys (arrow keys). Even if these keys are present, they may generate different codes than a standard PC keyboard does.

If your 386 system has a PC-style display, it will of course also have a PC-style keyboard. In addition, PC-scancode terminals support the full IBM keyboard. However, if you are using a standard ASCII terminal, you will need to use escape sequences to simulate the PC keys that aren't present on your keyboard.

Keyboard Equivalents in Merge

Table 5-1 lists the escape sequences used by Merge. These escape sequences are generated by pressing the ESC key, followed by the desired character.

As you can see, a couple of these keys (such as */PrtSc or Scroll Lock/Break) have two possible values. In order to use the shifted value, you must use the SHIFT escape sequence shown in Table 5-1, rather than the terminal's own shift key. For example, to use the PrtSc key, you must type ESC z ESC *. Likewise, to issue the PC reboot sequence, CTRL-ALT-DEL, you would type ESC c ESC a Esc d.

Keyboard Equivalents in VP/ix

VP/ix allows you to define keyboard equivalents on a terminal-by-terminal basis in a terminal configuration file. The keyboard assignments defined in the file for the Digital VT100 terminal are shown in Table 5-2. Note that any of these assignments can be redefined on a system-wide basis.

A Disk Drive By Any Other Name...

Both Merge and VP/ix create a virtual drive C: as part of the DOS environment. However, there are differences between the two programs in how this "drive" is actually implemented, where it is located in the UNIX file system, and how you access the rest of that file system.

In Merge, the root of C: corresponds to the root directory of the UNIX disk. Files created in the DOS environment are actually stored in the UNIX file system, and are accessible to other users of the UNIX system. Files created in the DOS environment can be read, copied or even modified by UNIX users. Likewise, from within Merge, you can access any part of the UNIX file system, under the illusion that files are really stored in a DOS directory structure.

In VP/ix, by contrast, the UNIX file system is accessed as drive Z:. The C: drive is a single file in the UNIX file system, which contains an actual DOS file system image. (This file is normally located in the directory */usr/vpix/defaults*. In addition, it is possible to create additional drives for each user.) This C: drive is used only for booting the virtual DOS enviroment. After booting, the default drive automatically changes to Z:.

Table 5-1. Keyboard Equivalents in Merge

PC KEY TO SIMULATE	KEYSTROKES
LEFT ARROW key	ESC f
RIGHT ARROW key	ESC g
UP ARROW key	ESC t
DOWN ARROW key	ESC v
HOME key	ESC h
END key	ESC e
PGUP key	ESC p
PGDN key	ESC q
INSERT key	ESC i
DELETE key	ESC d
5 key (numeric keypad)	ESC .
***/PRINT SCREEN** key	ESC *
SCROLL LOCK/BREAK key	ESC s
CAPS LOCK key	ESC k
NUM LOCK key	ESC n
Grey + key (numeric keypad)	ESC +
Grey - key (numeric keypad)	ESC -
F1 key	ESC 1
F2 key	ESC 2
F3 key	ESC 3
F4 key	ESC 4
F5 key	ESC 5
F6 key	ESC 6
F7 key	ESC 7
F8 key	ESC 8
F9 key	ESC 9
F10 key	ESC 0
ESC key (actual escape character)	ESC ESC
All keys released	ESC <space>
CTRL key	ESC c
ALT key	ESC a
LEFT SHIFT key	ESC z
RIGHT SHIFT key	ESC /

Table 5-2. VT100 Keyboard Equivalents in VP/ix

PC KEY TO SIMULATE	KEYSTROKES
LEFT ARROW key	← (ESC [D)
RIGHT ARROW key	→ (ESC [C)
UP ARROW key	↑ (ESC [A)
DOWN ARROW key	↓ (ESC [B)
HOME key	ESC h
END key	ESC e
PGUP key	ESC u
PGDN key	ESC d
INSERT key	ESC i
DELETE key	ESC l
5 key (numeric keypad)	CTRL-X 5
PR SCR key	ESC P
SCROLL LOCK key	CTRL-X s
BREAK key	CTRL-X b
CAPS LOCK key	CTRL-X c
NUM LOCK key	CTRL-X n
Grey + key (numeric keypad)	ESC +
Grey - key (numeric keypad)	ESC -
Grey . key (numeric keypad)	ESC .
F1 key	ESC 1
F2 key	ESC 2
F3 key	ESC 3
F4 key	ESC 4
F5 key	ESC 5
F6 key	ESC 6
F7 key	ESC 7
F8 key	ESC 8
F9 key	ESC 9
F10 key	ESC 0
ESC key (actual escape character)	ESC ESC
CTRL key	ESC r <any char> ESC R
ALT key	ESC t <any char> ESC T
LEFT SHIFT key	ESC f <any char> ESC F
RIGHT SHIFT key	ESC g <any char> ESC G
SYS REQ key	ESC 0 S (PF4)
BACK TAB key	ESC TAB

Other Virtual Drives

Some DOS programs don't take kindly to being stored in the UNIX file system. Some modify files in the root directory, which may not be desirable on a multi-user system. Others require that the program must be in the same directory as the files you work on. And finally, certain copy protected programs cannot be run from the UNIX file system.

To deal with these problems, Merge supplies three additional virtual drives. VP/ix allows additional drives to be created by the system administrator.

Private DOS File Systems

Under Merge, programs that require customized startup files in the root directory can be placed on the D: drive. This drive is just the same as C:, except that its root is the user's home directory. When a program is run from D:, it will look in the user's home directory (which it thinks is root) for any startup files, even if the program itself is stored elsewhere in the UNIX file system.

In VP/ix, drive H: works just like Merge's drive D:. In addition, users can be given a private copy of drive C: if they want their "virtual DOS machine" to use a private *autoexec.bat* or *config.sys* file. (When the system administrator creates a new VP/ix account, he or she is asked whether or not the user should have a private C: drive. If so, a copy of the C: file system is created in the user's home directory as well as in the standard location.)

Two For the Price of One

In Merge, drive J: corresponds exactly to drive C:. It is a clever hack, pure and simple, which lets you have two "current directories" at once, by treating each as if it were on a separate drive. Using this drive lets you fool a program such as WordStar, which requires data files to be kept in the same directory as the program.

When installing such a program, you would configure it to look for its overlays and configuration files on drive J:. To actually use the program, you would change directories on J: to the directory containing the program, and on C: to the directory where you want the data files to reside. Make sure you're logged to drive C:, then run the program on J:.

For example:

```
C> chdir j:\usr\ldbin\ws
C> chdir \usr\tim\book
C:\usr\tim\book> j:ws ch01
```

There is no analogue to drive J: in VP/ix.

Physical DOS Partitions

With Merge, programs that require a true DOS file system to run can be installed on a DOS-formatted partition on the hard disk, which can be accessed from Merge as drive E:.

In VP/ix, a DOS-formatted partition can be mapped to any drive letter. In addition, Interactive's implementation of UNIX for the 386, 386/ix, includes a facility called DOS-FSS that allows a DOS-formatted hard disk partition, or a DOS floppy, to be "mounted" as part of the UNIX file system. Users can thus access files stored on it through its pathname on drive Z:, just as they would any other files on the shared DOS/UNIX file system. This lets UNIX users use and share true DOS files even if no virtual PC's are running. (This feature relies on the UNIX V.3 File System Switch facility, and is not available with VP/ix running under older UNIX implementations.)

Floppy Drives

In both Merge and VP/ix, it is possible to use floppy drives on the system, just as you would with DOS. If another user is already using the drive, you will get an "Error Reading drive A:" prompt, just as you would in DOS if the door were open or the floppy not formatted correctly. More than one user cannot access the floppy drive at the same time.

In VP/ix, once a user has taken control of the drive, he or she must issue a special command to release it. It remains open for exclusive use until he or she quits VP/ix or releases it. This is also true of other limited hardware resources such as communications ports.

Comparing 386-based systems

Both DOS and UNIX can run on the 386 processor, but there is more to a system than the processor alone.

There are three different types of 386 systems on the market today.

- Very fast PCs (designed to run DOS and eventually OS/2), such as the Compaq 386, IBM's new PS/2 line, and a host of generic 386-based PCs.

- Departmental UNIX systems such as the Prime EXL-316 or the Convergent Server PC. These systems have been designed to run both UNIX and DOS, using the Locus and Interactive products described in this book.

- 386-based UNIX workstations. Unlike departmental systems, workstations are designed to be used by a single, very demanding user, even though they are nominally multi-user systems. Instead of the traditional multi-user system approach, workstations are designed to be networked. A workstation may have no disk drives (they access file servers on the UNIX network), but it always has its own processor and memory.

If you want a powerful, multi-tasking desktop machine for one or two people, you can soup up a 386-based PC. Here's our shopping list:

- **UNIX for the 386**. If you don't buy a system that already comes with UNIX, try SCO Xenix, Interactive Systems' 386/ix, or Microport's System V/386.

- **VP/ix or Merge**. Which one to buy depends on the version of UNIX you use. VP/ix is sold with Xenix and 386/ix, Merge with Microport System V/386.

- **Lots of memory**. Merge and VP/ix are resource hungry. They'll work best with at least 2 megabytes of memory for the first user, and 1 megabyte for each additional user.

- **A multi-user serial expansion board** so you can connect multiple ASCII terminals. Even better, get a fiber-optic link and memory-mapped terminals from Sun River Corp. Make sure the version of UNIX you're using supports the expansion board you buy!

Note that all this will cost you money—enough that you might instead want to consider a system such as the Prime EXL-316 or the Convergent Server PC. These machines have been designed expressly for multi-user operation, and will give you better performance for the price than a souped-up PC. This is especially important if you plan to support large numbers of users.

Figure 5-2
A Serial Expansion board lets you connect terminals to a PC running UNIX.

One area that these "departmental systems" have been optimized is in their handling of serial I/O. When many people are banging away on their keyboards at the same time, the load on the system is far greater than it might appear. The processor incurs an awful lot of overhead servicing the intermittent demands of multiple users.

So, for instance, the Prime EXL-316 includes an on-board 80186 processor in its serial controller. This offloads terminal input and output from the main processor and greatly improves overall system performance.

Buying a Macintosh II? Consider SoftPC

Merge and VP/ix only work on 386-based processors. They are ideal products for "departmental computers." But many research institutions prefer a network of high powered workstations from Sun, Apollo, DEC, HP, and most recently, Apple.

Sun is about to introduce a 386-based workstation that will run both DOS and UNIX. In addition, Apple's Macintosh II running A/UX (a version of UNIX) is expected to attract a wide group of new users to the UNIX workstation market. The Macintosh II running A/UX offers integration between UNIX and the popular Macintosh operating system. With a product called SoftPC from Insignia Solutions, the Macintosh II is also able to run off-the-shelf DOS applications.

The user is able to open one or more DOS windows on the workstation screen, and there run a complete DOS environment.

A product like SoftPC, which must emulate DOS in software, is necessarily slower than Merge or VP/ix, which can use the virtual-8086 mode of the 386 processor. However, if the workstation is dedicated to one user, performance may match or even exceed that of a 386-based machine with multiple DOS-under-UNIX users. Insignia Solutions claims XT performance on the Macintosh II, and AT performance on a Sun.

6
Merge and VP/ix: The Virtual DOS Environment

Merge and VP/ix allow you to run DOS and UNIX concurrently on a multi-user UNIX system based on the Intel 80286 or 80386 processor. Because they give former PC users continued access to familiar DOS application software, these products can help them make the transition into a UNIX system. Merge and VP/ix integrate the two environments so thoroughly that you can execute UNIX commands on DOS files and vice versa.

Many DOS users may at first be most comfortable using Merge or VP/ix to create a simulated DOS environment. Eventually, however, they may prefer to run DOS programs from the UNIX environment in order to gain the benefits of multi-tasking (even for DOS applications) as well as UNIX's own multi-user applications, such as electronic mail.

In this chapter, we'll talk about using the virtual DOS environment. In the next, we'll talk about using DOS commands from UNIX.

Creating a DOS Environment

With both Merge and VP/ix, the first step is to log on to the UNIX system, entering your name and password. Depending on how your account is set up, you might go right into the DOS environment, or you might go to the UNIX prompt. (To go to DOS, all the system administrator has to do is to include the appropriate command in your *.profile* or *.login* file.)

For the moment, let's assume that the administrator has left your account set up in such a way that you start out at the UNIX prompt.

If you are using Merge, you can create a DOS environment simply by entering **dos** at the system prompt. Merge then returns a standard DOS prompt.

```
$ dos
MS-DOS Version 3.1
C>
```

If you have an *autoexec.bat* file in your UNIX home directory, this file will be executed each time you enter the **dos** command, allowing you to tailor your own DOS environment.

To exit the DOS environment, and return to UNIX, you enter:

```
C> quit
```

If you are using VP/ix, the command to enter the DOS environment is **vpix**:

```
$ vpix
Welcome to MS-DOS Running in the VP/ix Environment
VP/ix Z:\>
```

The standard DOS prompt is preceded by the word VP/ix.

To exit VP/ix and return to UNIX, type **quit**.

Differences Between DOS and UNIX, Revisited

As discussed in Chapter 4 under PC-Interface, there are a number of minor differences between DOS and UNIX that the DOS user needs to be aware of while working in the Merge or VP/ix environment.

File Naming Conventions

The same problem of incompatible DOS and UNIX file names that was discussed in Chapter 4 also applies to Merge and VP/ix. UNIX names can be longer, may contain characters that are not legal in DOS filenames, and may have extensions longer than three characters.

Both Merge and VP/ix take the approach of mapping non-conforming UNIX filenames to legal DOS names and providing special commands to list the UNIX names or to convert them to DOS format.

Merge uses the same commands as PC-Interface: **udir** displays a combined directory listing showing both the mapped DOS name and the true UNIX name. The **uren** command allows you to rename a file, using as an argument a UNIX name.

In VP/ix, the **xdir** command performs the same function as Merge's **udir**. The DOS **rename** command can be used to rename a non-conforming UNIX file name, using the mapped file name.

Pathnames

As described in Chapter 5, Merge maps the entire DOS file system onto the UNIX file system. The root of the C: drive is the root of the UNIX file system. However, your current directory in DOS will be equivalent to the UNIX directory you were in when you issued the **dos** command to create the DOS environment.

You can access any file in the UNIX file system simply by typing its pathname, using the familiar DOS pathname syntax. The path will automatically be translated to its UNIX equivalent.

If you switch drives to D:, your home directory becomes the root of the virtual DOS file system.

```
C> dir \
Volume in drive C is UNIX
Directory of C:\

.    12-04-86    5:00p
..   11-23-86    3:00p
BIN  11-04-86    2:49p
ETC  10-23-86    1:45p
               .
               .
               .
USR10-18-86    4:39p

        10 File(s)        2341258 bytes free
C>D:
D>dir \
Volume in drive D is UNIX
Directory of D:\

sample.doc 1-22-88      9:23p
word.exe   1-12-88      1:23p
                .
                .
                .

        4 File(s)        2341258 bytes free
```

As shown in Figure 6-1, you cannot access any part of the UNIX file system "above" your home directory while logged to drive D:. Files must be accessed via drive C:. For example:

```
D:\USR\TIM>  dir c:\usr\dale
```

In VP/ix, the virtual drive Z: is mapped to the UNIX file system. Drive H: is mapped to the user's home directory. It is also possible for each user to establish a mapping between any drive letter and any directory in the UNIX file system. In addition, there is a C: drive which contains an actual DOS formatted file system, which is used chiefly for booting the virtual DOS machine rather than for file storage.

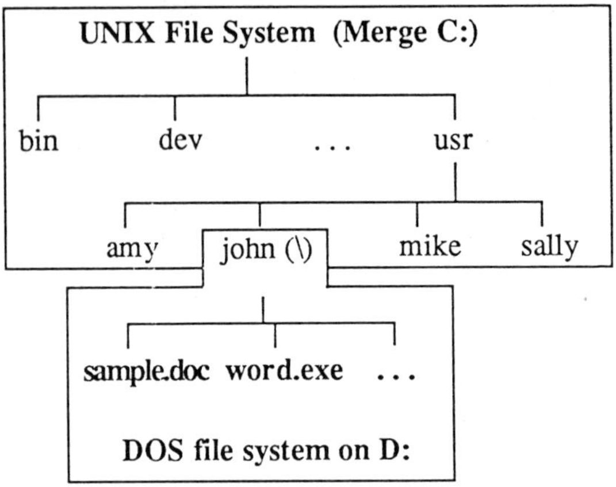

Figure 6-1
The UNIX file system as a whole is accessible as drive C:. The user's home directory corresponds to drive D:.

By default, you refer to files on a DOS drive by DOS pathname conventions. However, if you prefer to use the UNIX syntax, the **unixpath** command can be used to tell VP/ix to translate any UNIX pathnames and command switches you type to their DOS equivalents. The **dospath** command resets path interpretation to the default setting.

```
VP/ix Z:\>dir \bin\wc
Volume in drive Z is UNIX

Directory of Z:\bin
wc    13322     1-6-88     5:03p

      1 File(s)    9015296 bytes free VP/ix
Z:\>unixpath
VP/ix Z:/>dir /bin/wc
Volume in drive Z is UNIX

Directory of Z:/bin
wc    13322     1-6-88     5:03p

      1 File(s)    9015296 bytes free
```

Text File Formats

The Merge or VP/ix user must also face the fact of DOS/UNIX text file incompatibilities. UNIX terminates each line with a line-feed, while DOS uses a carriage-return/line-feed pair.

If you want to read a text file created with DOS using a UNIX program like the **vi** editor, or read a text file created under UNIX using a DOS editor or word processor, you will need to convert the file.

Merge uses the same text file conversion commands as PC-Interface, namely **unix2dos** and **dos2unix**. In VP/ix, there are corresponding commands called **utod** and **dtou**. However, a third command, called **lef** (for "Line Ending Filter") is more commonly used. The **lef** command copies either format to the other by analyzing the data in the source file, and picking the opposite format for the destination.

All of these commands take two arguments: the name of the existing file to be converted, and the name of a new file to be created using the alternate format. For example, to convert a UNIX text file called *unixfile* to a DOS text file called *dosfile.txt*:

```
VP/ix C:\> lef unixfile dosfile.txt
```

Alternatively, you can use the DOS copy command, with the switch **/d** to convert a UNIX file to DOS format, or **/u** to convert a DOS file to UNIX format. The following command will work just like the one shown above:

```
VP/ix C:\> copy unixfile dosfile.txt /d
```

The VP/ix **type** command is designed so that it will display both UNIX and DOS files correctly. No conversion is needed.

File Permissions

File access permissions are a foreign concept to DOS. However, as described in Chapter 4, they can be very important in a multi-user environment. Merge provides a version of the UNIX **chmod** command. However, it works a little differently than the UNIX version described in Chapter 3. The class of user to be affected by the command is specified first, followed by an equals sign and the desired permissions. For example, to set read/write permissions on *file.txt* , for both your group and all other users, you'd type:

```
C> chmod go=rw file.txt
```

The VP/ix **xdir** command works just like the DOS **dir** command, but shows in addition the file permissions (in square brackets), the UNIX user id and group id (in numeric form, contained in angle brackets), and the actual UNIX name of the file. The DOS name is shown in the first field, the UNIX equivalent in the last.

```
VP/ix Z:\>xdir \usr\tim\file.txt
Volume in Drive Z has no label
Directory of Z:\usr\tim

file.txt 1154 2-15-88 9:05a [rwr-r-] <150,5> file.txt
        1 File(s)   39834518 bytes free
```

Printing Files from DOS

You can use all of the standard DOS mechanisms for printing files with Merge or VP/ix. Your file will be sent to the UNIX print spooler, where it will print in its turn.

Let's say you created a DOS environment and wanted to print a file called *sales*. You could simply type:

```
C> print sales
```

Or, you could type:

```
C> copy sales lpt1
```

However, because the file is actually being sent to the UNIX print spooler, there are a few additional complications. UNIX treats a printer just like a file, and signals the end of data to be printed with an end-of-file character (CTRL-D in UNIX). DOS does not send any explicit signal when it is done with the printer.

In order to work properly with the UNIX print spooler, Merge stores the print output in a temporary file, and sends that file (complete with an end-of-file character) off to the printer either when you quit your DOS application, or when it has not received any more characters for at least 15 seconds. If you have an application that prints intermittently, or requires continuous access to the printer, this can cause your file to be printed as several different jobs.

It is possible to configure the length of Merge's print timeout with the **printer** command. You can set the timeout to zero, in which case output will be held in Merge's temporary file until you quit your application:

```
C> printer unix /t0
```

Or you can set the timeout to some number of seconds between 5 and 3600:

```
C> printer unix /t60
```

Or you can reset the default timeout:

```
C> printer unix /t
```

VP/ix takes a different approach, storing print data in a temporary file until you explicitly tell it to send the file to the UNIX spooler. When you are done printing from DOS, press the SYS REQ and ALT keys on the console, or equivalent keys on your terminal, and the VP/ix menu will appear:

```
VP/ix Version 1.1

(ESC) exit menu
(F)loppy release
(P)rinter flush
(Q)uit VP/ix
(R)eset VP/ix
(S)ound off
(U)nix shell
```

Simply press **P** to send the stored data to the print spooler.

Using UNIX Commands from DOS

Merge provides an **on** command similar to that used with PC-Interface. To run a UNIX command, you can either type:

```
C> on unix command
```

or you can link *on.exe* to various UNIX commands as described in Chapter 4.

In VP/ix, all of the UNIX utilities are already available, using a mechanism similar to that used with the PC-Interface/Merge ON utilities. There is a single DOS command (called **rununix.com** rather than **on.exe**) which is linked to all of the UNIX utility names.

These links are stored in the directory */usr/vpix/unixbin*. Additional commands you create can be stored in the directory *vpix/unixbin* which is created under your UNIX home directory when your VP/ix account is established. When you issue a UNIX command, it is this link to *rununix.com* that is actually executed. The DOS link invokes the corresponding UNIX command, and passes its arguments to it.

UNIX Pathnames and Switches

One thing you need to remember when using UNIX commands from VP/ix is to use the proper UNIX syntax for pathnames and command options. UNIX uses / to separate pathname elements, and - to introduce a command option. So, for example, you would type:

```
VP/ix Z:\> ls -l /usr/bin
```

to get a long listing of the UNIX directory */usr/bin*.

Using Custom UNIX Commands from DOS

When a VP/ix account is created, links are created between *rununix.com* and the names of all standard UNIX utilities. These links are stored in the */usr/vpix/unixbin* directory, and that directory is added to your DOS search path.

But what if you have custom UNIX programs or shell scripts that you would like to be able to access from DOS? It is fairly simple to add them to your DOS repertoire.

First, make sure that the custom command is located somewhere in your UNIX search path. Then create a link between *rununix.com* and a file with the same name as your custom program, plus a *.com* extension. Place this link in your *vpix/unixbin* directory.

For example, assume that you had created a UNIX program and stored it in the file */usr/local/bin/doit*. The following UNIX commands will make the command accessible from VP/ix:

```
$ cd $HOME/vpix/unixbin
$ ln rununix.com doit.com
```

Now, when the DOS user types **doit**, he or she will actually be calling **rununix.com**, which will traverse the UNIX search path and find the real doit program.

If you want a custom program to be accessible to all VP/ix users, the link should be placed in */usr/vpix/unixbin* instead of in your personal *unixbin* subdirectory. Note of course that UNIX file permissions may allow only the system administrator to add programs to the system-wide *vpix* directory.

The procedure for adding custom programs to the Merge environment is the same as that described for PC-Interface in Chapter 4.

Configuring the DOS Environment

On a DOS system, users are able to customize their environment by running commands and setting system variables in an *autoexec.bat* file that is executed automatically each time the system is booted. In addition, system variables can be defined in the *config.sys* file.

The Merge and VP/ix environments also support the use of these configuration files. However, due to the increased complexity of these environments, there are a number of other configuration mechanisms as well.

The *autoexec.bat* File

In Merge, the DOS environment is initialized by a system-wide *autoexec.bat* file, followed by a secondary *autoexec.bat* in the user's home directory. Users can add commands to their local copy of the file in order to customize their private DOS environment. Likewise, there is both a global and a private copy of *config.sys*.

When you enter the DOS environment, the system-wide file is executed first, followed by the local version.

In VP/ix, there is only a single system-wide copy of each of these files. However, users can be given private copies of the C: drive, in which case they will control their own *autoexec.bat* and *config.sys* file.

The *vpix.cnf* File

In VP/ix, it is possible for users to have private DOS drives. A separate C: drive can be created in your home directory (or any other location) when your VP/ix account is created.

Which drives the user can access (as well as the UNIX device names corresponding to various other resources such as communications ports) is defined in a file in the user's UNIX home directory called *vpix/vpix.cnf*.

DOS Options, DOSOPT and DOSADMIN

In addition to the standard DOS configuration mechanisms, Merge allows you to set a variety of conditions using command-line options to the **dos** command you use to fire up a DOS environment.

You can use the **dosopt** command to set up environment defaults that will be used each time you enter the DOS Merge environment, as well as defaults for individual applications. For the faint of heart, there is a menu-driven command called **dosadmin** that allows you to set some of the most important environment options. Both of these commands must be run from UNIX rather than from the DOS environment.

Environment options include the amount of memory to allocate for DOS, whether or not to use *autoexec.bat* and/or *config.sys* files, the location of alternate *autoexec.bat* and/or *config.sys* files, whether print spooling should be enabled, and whether any UNIX devices should be attached for exclusive use by DOS.

Application-specific options include the amount of memory to be assigned to the application, whether or not to attach devices to the application, whether it is stream-oriented or display-oriented, and so on. These options are most relevant when you are using DOS commands from the UNIX shell, and are discussed in the next chapter. (For example, the amount of memory allocated to an application needs to be specified only if the application is being run outside the DOS environment.)

Most of these options are not necessary for the average Merge user. However, they do provide a great amount of control for advanced users.

Environment values set with **dosopt** or **dosadmin** are stored in a number of configuration files. System-wide defaults for the DOS environment are stored in the file */etc/dosenv.def*, while system-wide application defaults are stored in */etc/dosapp.def*. Equivalent local files are stored in each user's home directory, and allow each user to set his or her own default values.

7

Merge and VP/ix: Running DOS from UNIX

In the preceding chapter, we showed you how to create a DOS environment after logging on to a UNIX host. This is ideal for DOS users who want to continue to work in a familiar environment on a UNIX-based machine. They will gain the benefits of UNIX print spooling and system management services, and may be able to use UNIX utilities on DOS files. However, they will not be able to take real advantage of the multi-tasking capabilities of UNIX unless they begin to work with the UNIX shell.

In addition to creating a complete DOS environment, Merge and VP/ix allow you to run DOS programs directly from UNIX. Doing so has many advantages. First of all, you can use UNIX's multi-tasking to run multiple DOS programs at once. Secondly, you can use UNIX's interactive programs such as electronic mail and can pipe data between DOS and UNIX programs.

Using DOS Commands from UNIX

Both Merge and VP/ix can distinguish a DOS command from a UNIX command, so you can execute DOS commands directly from the UNIX prompt.

For example, to display the files in your current directory, instead of typing the **ls** command, you could type the DOS equivalent:

```
$ dir
```

This command produces a DOS-style display.

Some Things to Watch Out For

With Merge, when you enter DOS commands directly from UNIX, you must use UNIX syntax for path separators (/) and for command options (–). For example, to move a file called *addresses* from one directory to another, you'd type

```
$ ren addresses /usr/julie/addresses
```

instead of

```
$ ren addresses \usr\julie\addresses
```

VP/ix, by contrast, allows you to use the standard DOS syntax. However, you need to be aware that both \ and / (the DOS command switch and pathname separators) have special meanings to the UNIX shell. (\ is an escape character, which means to take the following special character literally, and / is the pathname separator for UNIX.) As a result, you should use single quotes to insulate all special characters in a DOS command line from interpretation by the shell.

```
$ dir '\usr\julie /w'
```

In both Merge and VP/ix, you must also type DOS commands in lower case while working in the UNIX environment.

In addition, you need to be aware of complications when using file naming metacharacters such as * and ?. In UNIX, the shell, not the application program, expands and interprets these characters. This can lead to problems with DOS commands. For example, the command:

```
$ copy *.txt a:
```

translates in UNIX to the command:

```
$ copy file1.txt file2.txt ... a:
```

Unlike its UNIX equivalent, **cp**, the DOS **copy** command does not allow multiple individually-specified source arguments, so this command will fail.

The answer, once again, is to quote the command line arguments. You can also use the backslash character to "quote" a single special character. The following two command lines will work equally well:

```
$ copy '*.txt a:'
$ copy \*.txt a:
```

Of course, you could also just get used to the UNIX **cp** command, and use the DOS programs that have no UNIX equivalents—your applications.

Piping Data Between DOS and UNIX Programs

A pipe is a mechanism for passing data between programs. Pipes are one of the most useful features of UNIX, and have been added to all DOS versions later than 2.0.

Pipes allow you to use programs as *filters*. That is, you can use one program to limit, organize or transform the output of another. For example, to obtain a sorted listing of a DOS directory you might type:

```
$ dir | sort
```

Pipes have even greater usefulness in UNIX because so many commands are stream-oriented. For example, the **sed** and **awk** commands provide complete editing and database manipulation capabilities that can work on data in a pipe.

Both Merge and VP/ix allow you to pipe data between DOS and UNIX programs, so you can use stream-oriented programs from both environments interchangeably.

DOS Commands You Can't Use in UNIX

There are a few DOS commands that have no meaning in the UNIX environment. For example, you can't run **chkdsk**, **format**, **sys**, **fdisk** or **ship** commands on the shared DOS/UNIX file system. (You can't run these commands from inside the virtual DOS environment either.) In Merge, the merged file system is not a true DOS file system, but a view of the UNIX file system.

In VP/ix, C: is a true DOS file system, but Z: is not. You can run **chkdsk** on C:, but not on Z:. You can't run **format**, **fdisk** or **ship**, since these commands affect the physical disk.

In both Merge and VP/ix, you can use these commands (plus **diskcopy**) on a DOS-formatted floppy disk.

You also can't run commands like **prompt**, **path** or **set** from UNIX, since they only affect the DOS environment, which is not in effect at the time.

Finally, there are commands that are so closely equivalent in DOS and UNIX to be unavailable. In Merge, these commands include **mkdir**, **rmdir** and **chdir**. (All three are available in VP/ix.)

In other cases, two commands of the same name are available. These commands include **sort**, **find**, **more** and (in VP/ix) **cd**. You can really get confused if you forget which version of the command you're using. For example, in DOS, typing **cd** without any arguments reports the current working directory. In UNIX, the equivalent command is **pwd**; **cd** without any arguments takes you back to your home directory.

You must specify an explicit pathname if you want to use the DOS version. For example, to use the DOS **sort** command in Merge instead of the UNIX version, you'd type:

```
$ /usr/dbin/sort myfile
```

Another trick, which should work in Merge (but is not necessary in VP/ix) is to type the full name of the DOS program, including the extension. For example:

```
$ sort.exe myfile
```

In VP/ix, which command will be executed is controlled by the standard UNIX **PATH** variable, as well as a new variable called DOSPATH. DOSPATH is described in the next section.

Making Additional DOS Programs Accessible From UNIX

Both DOS and UNIX use the concept of the search path to specify where the command interpreter should look to find commands to execute. However, there is another, less obvious mechanism that is also at work. DOS programs are identified as executable by one of the extensions **.com**, **.exe**, or **.bat**. UNIX programs are marked executable as part of the file permissions attribute set with the **chmod** command.

What this means is that in DOS, when you type the command **mycommand**, DOS actually looks through the search path for a file called *mycommand.com*, *mycommand.exe* or *mycommand.bat*. The standard UNIX shell actually looks for a file called *mycommand*, and will not recognize the file if it has one of the required DOS extensions.

Merge and VP/ix have taken different approaches to solving this problem. In Merge, part of the standard installation procedure for any DOS programs to be executed from the UNIX shell is to make a link between the DOS name (with extension), and a UNIX name (without extension). As described previously, a link allows the same file to be accessed by two different names, and takes up no more disk space than a single copy of the file. Links are created with the **ln** command.

System-wide DOS commands are kept in the directory */usr/dbin*, and additional applications are loaded into */usr/ldbin*. So, for example, to make the DOS program **mycommand.exe** available from UNIX (under Merge), you would type the following command:

```
$ ln mycommand.exe /usr/ldbin/mycommand
```

In addition to the system-wide command directory, you may have a local command directory that is also added to your search path. In Merge, each user account includes a local *dbin* directory under the home directory.

In VP/ix, the Bourne shell and C shell have both been modified to understand DOS command name conventions, so it is not necessary to link a *.bat*, *.exe*, or *.com* file to the equivalent name without the extensions.

Instead, VP/ix users have a new enviroment variable called *DOSPATH*, which is a list of directories in the same format as PATH. DOSPATH must always be a strict subset of PATH for a given user. By default, DOSPATH includes the directories */usr/vpix/dosbin* and *vpix/dosbin* in each user's home directory. When a VP/ix shell is searching for a file, it searches directories in the order specified by the PATH variable, as usual. However, if a directory in PATH is also in DOSPATH, the shell appends *.bat*, *.exe*, and *.com* suffixes to the name, one at a time, and searches for those names before searching for the simple unsuffixed name. If it finds a *.bat*, *.com*, or *.exe*, it executes VP/ix with the matching name as a parameter.

Thus, no links are required to install a DOS program under VP/ix.

Multi-tasking

Multi-tasking is probably the greatest benefit that you have in running DOS programs from the UNIX shell rather than from the virtual DOS environment. UNIX allows more than one program to run at the same time, sharing CPU time and disk access between a user's multiple processes just as it shares resources among multiple users.

Background Processing

As described in Chapter 3, it is possible to run UNIX programs in the background. They continue to run, but return the keyboard and screen to you so you can do other work. To run a program in the background, you simply place an ampersand (&) at the end of the command line. If the program normally sends output to the screen, you should redirect it to a file, or pipe it to the print spooler.

In the standard UNIX environment, background processing is most useful for stream-oriented programs whose output is redirected to a file or printer. For example, the **troff** program formats an ASCII file marked up with typesetting instructions and converts it into a format that will drive a phototypesetter or laser printer.

This process takes a few minutes (especially for a large file), and is most productively run in the background so you can do other things.

It is not possible to run a display-oriented program (such as the UNIX **vi** editor, or a DOS application like 1-2-3) in the background. Since the program takes over the screen display, and requires input from the user to operate, there is no point in running it in the background—at least on a standard terminal.

Multiple Screens on Memory Mapped Terminals

However, if you are using a memory-mapped terminal (i.e., the PC console, or a PC-style graphics terminal), you ***can*** run even display-oriented programs in the background! (See Chapter 5 for a discussion of different types of terminals.) These terminals support multiple "screens" that you can switch between with a "hot key" combination (CTRL-SYS REQ in Merge; and in VP/ix under 386/ix, ALT-SYS REQ followed by F1, F2, ... for whichever screen you want from 1 to 8).

(This switch-screen capability is actually not a feature of either Merge or VP/ix, but a feature of the UNIX operating system itself. As a result, it may operate differently depending on which underlying version of UNIX is being used.)

When you combine this switch-screen capability with UNIX background processing, you have a mechanism for multi-tasking even display-oriented applications. Whenever you start a display-oriented program such as 1-2-3 from a memory-mapped terminal, Merge or VP/ix will create a new screen for it. If you run the program in the background, you can switch screens to work with other applications or the UNIX shell.

For example, if you type:

```
$ 123 &
```

1-2-3 will be run in the background as far as UNIX is concerned, but since you get a new "screen" to work with, you can work with the program as if it were in the foreground. Simply press CTRL-SYS REQ to switch back to the UNIX shell.

DOS users may have trouble getting used to the idea that the program is still working, even when it is not visible. Switching screens is not like using a "hot key" in a DOS application to temporarily get back to DOS. You can do that only when the program is not working. You can start a huge worksheet recalculating or printing, switch to another screen, and have the background program finish the job while you're doing other work.

In Merge, you can have up to four different "screens" going at the same time. Pressing CTRL-SYS REQ will flip through each of the screens in turn.

You can even run an entire virtual DOS environment in the background on a separate screen:

```
$ dos &
```

Using VP/ix with Interactive's 386/ix, you don't need to run programs in the background to get the benefit of multiple screens. Each virtual screen is treated as if it were a separate terminal by 386/ix.

When you first switch to a new screen, you will see a UNIX login prompt. Once you've logged in to multiple screens, you can switch from one to the other by pressing ALT-SYS REQ followed by a function key from F1 to F8. (386/ix lets you select any one of 8 screens by number, rather than by flipping through each screen in sequence.)

Logging Out From Multiple Screens

In Merge, when you exit from a program that is running on its own screen, you will be returned to the "parent" screen—the one you were using when you started the program. However, if you terminate the original UNIX login session on the parent screen, all subsidiary processes will also be terminated.

You need to watch out that you don't work in an application such as 1-2-3, switch back to the UNIX screen without saving your file, and then log out. It is probably a good safety precaution always to save your work before you switch screens.

Multi-tasking with Subshells

While it is true that you can't run a display-oriented program in the background on an ASCII or PC Scancode terminal, you *can* escape from the program and get back to the UNIX shell. This shell is called a subshell, since it is a distinct process from the original login shell.

Again, unlike the DOS escapes built into many DOS applications, an escape to a UNIX shell will allow the application to run in the background. So, for example, you could be running a time-consuming database sort, spawn a subshell, and then run another DOS or UNIX program. The sort may well be done by the time you get back to your database application.

The difference between multi-tasking with subshells versus multiple screens is that you can't switch between the subshell and the original application. You must terminate the subshell in order to get back to your application.

In Merge, the keystroke combination ESC CTRL-F will create a UNIX subshell on an ASCII terminal. CTRL-SYS REQ CTRL-F will do the trick on a scancode terminal. In VP/ix, press SYS REQ to display the VP/ix menu, then type **U** to create a UNIX shell, or, more simply, just type **sh** at the VP/ix prompt.

In either Merge or VP/ix, type **exit** to terminate the subshell and return to your application.

Note that you can create a UNIX subshell from within the virtual DOS environment as well as from within a DOS application run from the UNIX prompt.

Working With Floppies

From within the virtual DOS environment, you can access files and programs on floppies just as easily as you can those on the virtual DOS disk.

However, programs invoked from the UNIX shell expect to treat the floppy as a UNIX device. In UNIX, floppies can be *mounted* (made a part of the UNIX file system), or they can be read and written directly by backup programs such as **tar** and **cpio**.

In Merge, DOS programs run from UNIX can read or write from a DOS-formatted floppy disk just as they would if run from DOS. However, running a DOS program from a floppy is a little more complicated.

To copy a file to a DOS-formatted disk, you could simply use the **copy** command (making sure to quote the command line arguments):

```
$ copy '*.txt a:'
```

(If you are transferring text files to a DOS floppy, you probably first want to convert them to DOS textfile format with the **unix2dos** command.)

To run a DOS program contained on a floppy disk, you can use a variation on the same **dos** command that you use to enter the virtual DOS environment. The +c option says to pass the following command line directly to **command.com**. For example, to run a copy of 1-2-3 from a floppy in the A: drive, you'd type:

```
$ dos +c a:123
```

(If this seems a little awkward, remember that while you can quote command line arguments, you can't quote the command name itself. If you were to type **a:123** at the shell prompt, the shell would look through the search path for a file called *a:123*.)

If you're using VP/ix, there are two mechanisms that allow you to access a DOS-formatted floppy from the UNIX shell. DOS-FSS (DOS File System Support) allows a DOS floppy or hard disk partition to be mounted as part of the UNIX file system. Files on the floppy can then be accessed just as if they were UNIX files and directories. However, the programs needed to mount a file system are generally restricted to the system administrator, so DOS-FSS is generally limited to cases in which users want access to a DOS floppy for an extended period of time. (This facility is not designed for routine file transfer between DOS and UNIX so much as to allow programs stored on a DOS partition or floppy to be accessed by UNIX users.)

The **dossette** utilities allow users to create a temporary DOS environment on a floppy.

```
$ dossette

A>
```

Unlike VP/ix, **dossette** does not give access to a true DOS environment, but actually mimics the action of DOS commands, so the available commands are more limited. Common file operations like **dir**, **copy**, **rename**, **erase**, **format** and **cd** are supported, as well as a **help** command. The special **get** and **put** commands allow you to transfer files from the DOS floppy to the UNIX file system or the

Merge and VP/ix in a Mixed Network

We've said that you need an Intel 386-based system to enjoy the benefits of Merge or VP/ix. This is not quite true.

You do need at least one 386-based system to run these products—but in a networked environment, that one machine can act as a "DOS server" for all connected machines.

All that users connected to other UNIX machines on the network need to do is to use the standard TCP/IP **rlogin** utility (or even an asynchronous communications program like TERM) to log in to the 386-based system. They can run DOS programs from there.

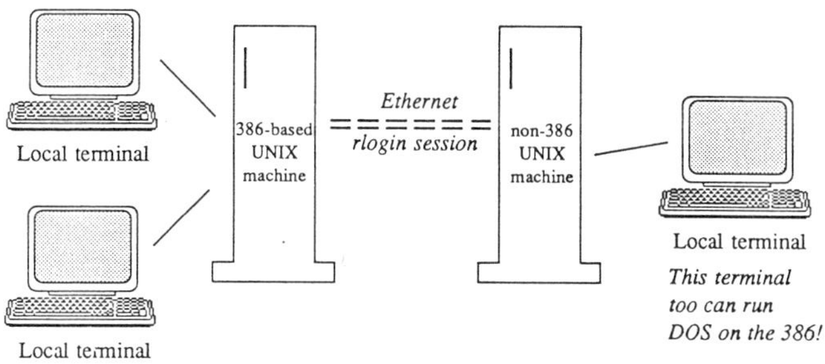

Of course, you should be aware that Merge and VP/ix make heavy use of system resources. A 386-based system can typically only support six concurrent DOS users under UNIX.

❖

reverse, automatically performing any necessary text file conversions. The **q** command exits **dossette**. You can't run DOS applications from a floppy with **dossette**.

You can also use any of the **dossette** commands in a "batch mode" from the UNIX prompt, simply by prepending the word **dos** to the appropriate command name. For example:

```
$ dosget a:/dosunix/ch01.txt ch01.txt
```

will copy the file *ch01.txt* (chapter one of this book) from the directory *dosunix* on drive A: to the current UNIX directory.

A

How the Magic Is Accomplished

This appendix is adapted from the article, "Two That Tango on the 80386," by Ken Sarno of Interactive Systems, which originally appeared in the January 1988 issue of Unix Review. *It is reprinted by permission of the author and the editors of* Unix Review.

Many in the UNIX community saw the announcement of the Intel 80386 microprocessor as the long-awaited light at the end of the Intel architecture tunnel. With its high level of performance, its 32-bit registers and addressing, and its on-chip support for a large, demand-paged virtual memory, the 80386 is the first Intel microprocessor whose architecture helps, rather than hinders, the portability of UNIX and its applications.

Intel's latest offering, moreover, has an additional plus that is helping it become one of the most important forces in the UNIX marketplace: the "virtual 8086 mode" ("V8086" for short), a new operating mode that—when properly supported by system software—allows the creation of multi-user DOS-under-UNIX systems.

(It is interesting to note that OS/2, the new, 80286-oriented, single-user, multitasking operating system from Microsoft and IBM, is closer in design to UNIX than it is to DOS. It retains backward compatibility with DOS by running one DOS application at a time in a real-mode "compatibility box" that somewhat resembles OS/Merge. In a sense, then, OS/2 provides DOS-under-something-like-UNIX.)

Several products that use V8086 mode to integrate DOS into multiprogramming environments were announced soon after the 80386 itself. Two of them are multi-user DOS-under-UNIX products: VP/ix, from Interactive Systems Corporation and Phoenix Technologies Ltd., and Merge 386, from Locus Computing Corporation.

This appendix discusses the major influence the V8086 mode has had on DOS-under-UNIX technology, as well as a few of the technical issues that have been encountered in using this mode to create a multi-user, DOS-under-UNIX environment on the 80386. Implementation examples are drawn from VP/ix, since that is the DOS-under-UNIX system with which the author is most familiar.

Virtual 8086 Mode

Compatibility with earlier designs (for good or ill) has been a hallmark of Intel processors, and the 80386 is no exception. The 80386 has four different operating modes. One is the new 32-bit mode that makes the 80386 a good UNIX machine. The other three are 16-bit modes whose only purpose is to provide for backward compatibility.

In "32-bit protected mode," the 80386 is a much more powerful device than any of its Intel predecessors. At 32 bits, its computational registers are double in size, and Intel's restrictions on register usage have been relaxed so that, for example, more register variables now are available in C programs. The familiar segmented Intel architecture still is visible, but is easy to overlook: each 32-bit "segment" is a separate 4 GB demand-paged virtual address space. The paging hardware needed to manage these large virtual spaces is on-chip, including a translation look-aside buffer that caches the most recently used page table entries to achieve added performance. As a result of these and other enhancements, the 32-bit mode of the 80386 is well able to support UNIX and other demanding operating systems.

The other three 80386 modes are all compatibility modes. By default, the chip runs in "real mode," a 16-bit mode that closely mimics the operation of the original Intel 8086 chip. Real mode makes no use of the 80386's more advanced facilities, but it does allow the chip to serve as a CPU in a PC-compatible environment.

In "16-bit protected mode," the 80386 is a strict superset of its 16-bit ancestor, the 80286. Operating systems written for the protected mode of the 80286, such as OS/2 or earlier versions of UNIX and Xenix, run unchanged on the 80386 if the surrounding hardware is compatible. Newer operating systems written for the 80386 can easily support a concurrent mix of 32-bit and older 16-bit protected mode applications; the 80386 versions of both UNIX System V.3 and Xenix run the 16-bit binaries (which is to say the compiled, or "object," programs) from their respective 80286 versions—along with 32-bit programs. Mode transitions between the 16-bit and 32-bit protected modes cost nothing in software overhead.

Intel now has added a new twist to backward compatibility in the 80386 by including a *fourth* operating mode: the "virtual 8086 mode," a hybrid that blends some of the operating characteristics of the real mode with some that are more associated with the protected modes—along with a few additional features of its own. The intent in producing V8086 mode was to allow real-mode programs that normally own an entire machine (such as DOS and its applications) to execute within the confines of a privilege-protected, multitasking, virtual-memory system such as UNIX.

It is this virtual 8086 mode that makes DOS-under-UNIX systems on the 80386 radically different from all of their predecessors, because it allows DOS to run in a *virtual* machine, rather than in a real one. DOS programs in previous systems ran in real mode on a "real" PC. In software-only, 80286-based systems such as OS/Merge and OS/2, the 80286 runs in protected mode when 80286 host applications are running, but returns to real mode whenever the hosted DOS environment is running. In coprocessor systems, meanwhile, DOS programs run on a dedicated 80286 processor board that always runs in real mode and duplicates much of the hardware found in an IBM PC.

Running DOS in real mode has two consequences. First, it allows only one instance of DOS to run in the system, because real mode depends on physical addresses. Second, in software-only implementations (but not coprocessors), real mode poses a major threat to the integrity of the host system. A real-mode program that, for example, accidentally scrambles a critical interrupt vector will crash UNIX when run under OS/Merge, and will bring down OS/2 when run in its "compatibility box." The reason for this is that in real mode none of the normal system protections are in effect.

By contrast, under VP/ix and Merge 386, DOS runs in a virtual environment. There is no DOS dependence on a given area of physical memory, and no direct DOS access to system-critical resources such as timers and interrupt hardware. Many virtual DOS environments can run simultaneously, and none will threaten the integrity of the system or of other applications. Because each virtual DOS environment can be implemented as a UNIX process, processor time can be divided fairly among UNIX and DOS activities; that means DOS no longer can "hog" the whole machine to the exclusion of UNIX processing. And because of the processing throughput of the 80386, several DOS processes can share the system with UNIX, and still deliver performance comparable to an 80286 AT-class machine for most applications.

In addition, since the environment in V8086 mode is virtualized, it can be ported to any 80386-based hardware platform. For example, with the help of VP/ix, DOS applications written for the IBM PC can be run on systems that use the Multibus architecture, as well as on other 80386-based architectures.

Requirements of a Virtual PC

A real IBM PC running DOS is a layered environment (see Figure A-1). The lowest layer consists of the processor, the machine's memory, and its LSI peripheral chips. On the next layer, we find the BIOS (Basic Input/Output System), which provides software interfaces to most of the PC's peripheral devices. Above that is DOS, which provides another set of software interfaces to file and memory management services, as well as to the BIOS. On the uppermost layer rests the DOS application program, which *should* communicate with the hardware only through DOS and the BIOS. Not all applications do, though. Applications that obey the published BIOS and DOS interface specifications are called "well-behaved." By definition, this includes all UNIX programs because they run in a protected environment, and thus can't get away with breaking the rules.

Unfortunately, if you went to your local software store and threw a dart into the IBM PC section, your chances of striking a completely well-behaved DOS program would be very slim indeed. The overwhelming majority of DOS programs have been written to run on the older, 8088-based IBM PCs, where there aren't many compute cycles to be had. DOS programmers aren't willing to squander what precious cycles they do have to issue calls, for example, to a DOS or BIOS routine so as to write a character to the screen when their application can instead simply access the screen directly. As a result, they ignore all the published rules and available interfaces, and manipulate display memory and/or device controller registers directly from their application code. And this doesn't even exhaust

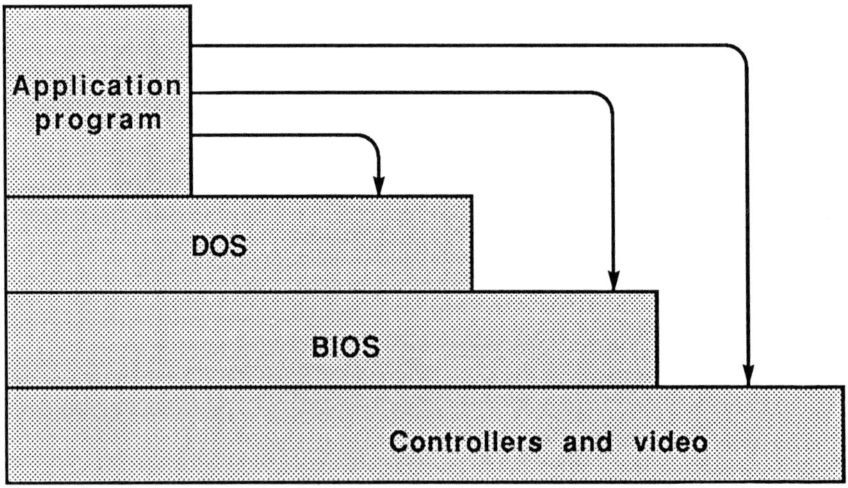

Figure A-1
PC applications can bypass the standard DOS and BIOS interfaces to access the hardware layer directly, since there is no privilege-based protection in real mode. Programs that exploit this fact are called "ill-behaved," and are harder to deal with in a hosted DOS environment.

the reasons for breaking the rules: most DOS programs also exhibit one or more forms of "bad behavior" for fast screen output, diskette-based copy protection, interrupt-driven asynchronous communications (which aren't available via the BIOS), and so forth.

Some programs, in fact, are so ill-behaved that they won't run properly (or at all) in an emulated environment. For example, DOS programs that go into 80286 protected mode can't be emulated in virtual 8086 mode. Programs with very strict real-time requirements may not work because they must share the processor with other activities. But, in general—"ill-behaved" or not—programs must be kept working, and therefore DOS-under-UNIX systems must tolerate both "good" and "ill" behavior by providing to its "client" DOS applications an emulation of all three lower layers: hardware, BIOS, and DOS itself.

To detail all the emulation methods used in creating a virtual PC would require more space than is available here. Instead, we'll focus on three of the most important and interesting aspects of emulation, and how they are handled by VP/ix:

- *The Underlying Virtual PC Mechanism.* We'll look at how V8086 mode works and how VP/ix uses it within the bounds of UNIX to create an 8086 virtual-machine process.

- *Emulation of the DOS File System.* A consideration is included of how DOS applications running in a virtual machine are able to process UNIX files as though they were DOS files, thereby eliminating the need for a DOS partition on the UNIX host's disk. This is the most important emulation of the services always accessed through a "well-behaved" interface.

- *Emulation of the DOS Display on Terminals.* One aspect of 80386 DOS-under-UNIX products that distinguish them from earlier DOS-under-UNIX products is that they're capable of supporting several DOS users at the same time. Of course, only one person can use the console display; the remaining users must run their DOS applications on simulated PC displays that actually are conventional RS-232 serial terminals. We'll see how VP/ix accommodates this most important form of programmed "ill-behavior."

Virtual PC Mechanisms

Virtual 8086 mode is far from a full virtual-machine environment for DOS programs. It provides only a couple of basic hardware facilities that a DOS virtual machine can't exist without:

- *Simulation of several real-mode address spaces in virtual memory.* All 8086 programs and—by extension—all real-mode programs on any Intel CPU, assume that the addresses they manipulate internally correspond to physical locations. In V8086 mode, the 80386 uses its paging unit to perform virtual-to-physical translation on all "physical" memory addresses generated by real-mode code. Several 1 MB virtual 8086 address spaces can exist at the same time, and—as under any other virtual memory scheme—each can be demand-paged in and out of arbitrary physical memory locations (see Figure A-2).

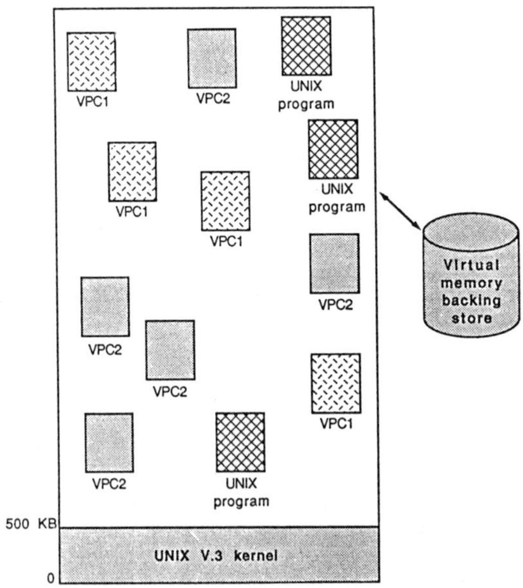

Figure A-2
Because virtual 8086 mode provides address translation, VP/ix virtual PCs are simply UNIX processes in demand-paged virtual memory. Shown are two virtual PCs sharing virtual memory with one ordinary UNIX process. Small squares represent 4 KB pages.

- ***Trapping of privileged instructions.*** **There are no different privilege levels in real mode; any program can do anything it wants, whether that's to format the hard disk, disable interrupts, enter a tight loop, or whatever. In V8086 mode, however, programs are subject to the same restrictions as the least-privileged protected-mode program. Any attempt to perform hardware-level I/O, or to change the state of the processor's interrupt-enable flag causes a trap out of the V8086 mode into protected mode. Software interrupts and other privileged instructions also cause traps.**

V8086 mode, can thus be summarized as follows: it allows 8086 programs to use virtualized, real-mode addresses at a harmless, low privilege level. The first challenge in implementing a DOS-under-UNIX facility on the 80386, then, is the integration of this feature into the base UNIX operating system.

The Virtual 8086 Monitor

A trap out of the V8086 mode transfers control to a protected-mode program or routine that Intel calls the V8086 mode monitor. It is the monitor's job to analyze the reason for the trap, to emulate the trapped operation, and to return control to the V8086 mode. This sounds simple enough, but it can cover a lot of territory in a DOS-under-UNIX environment. Traps can occur for reasons ranging from the occurrence of DOS system calls, which must be translated into corresponding UNIX calls, to "disable interrupts" instructions, which do nothing but set an emulation flag in the monitor.

It is the monitor's job to virtualize, or mimic, the behavior of the environment being emulated by intercepting and translating every attempt by its client DOS applications to "touch" lower layers:

- If programs in the virtual machine require a file system that's different from the host's file system, the monitor must translate the client application's virtual file-system calls into semantics appropriate to the host's real file system.

- If DOS programs write directly to a virtualized display memory, the monitor must make sure that changes to this memory appear on the user's real display, even if that display is a dumb terminal or an X Window.

- When client applications try to access the registers of peripheral controllers directly, which often is the case under DOS, the monitor must manage a software model of the corresponding virtual device, causing the client application to perceive "correct" behavior on its end, while using the host's real hardware facilities to achieve the desired result on the other. If this portion of the emulation is complete enough, DOS applications, including those described as "ill-behaved," can run on 80386 systems with non-PC architectures (machines using Multibus, for example).

The monitor's implementation is divided between the kernel code and user-mode code. Some kernel "hooks" are unavoidable: UNIX has no native understanding, for instance, of how to put the processor into the V8086 mode. Certain memory-management tricks have to be played in the interest of performance, and these can only be performed in the kernel. Time-critical emulation functions, such as the disassembly of the most frequent trap-causing instructions, must also be performed in the kernel. Large, slow, or infrequently used emulation code, however, is best kept *out* of the kernel, especially the UNIX V.3 kernel, which is large enough already.

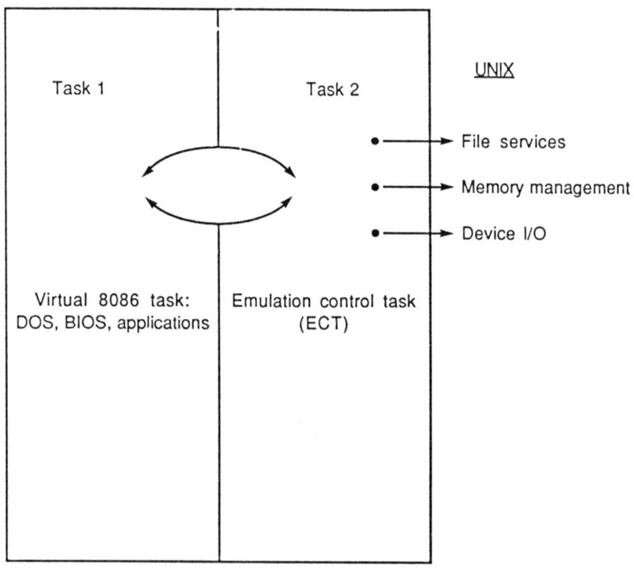

Figure A-3
A VP/ix virtual PC is a pair of tasks that the UNIX kernel treats as a single process. One task runs in virtual 8086 mode, the other in 32-bit protected mode. The protected mode Emulation Control Task uses UNIX system calls to provide the virtual PC's interface to the UNIX system.

The VP/ix Virtual Machine

The 80386 inherited from the 80286 a silicon task-switching mechanism that fits well with virtual 8086 mode. The CPU chip can switch quickly between two tasks by automatically saving the old task's state into a special data structure and loading the state of the new task from a second, similar structure. During the switch, the processor can change modes—it might go from 32-bit protected mode to virtual 8086 mode, for instance—without incurring any additional overhead. VP/ix uses the hardware multi-tasking feature to keep as much of the monitor as possible in user space, and yet allow efficient control transfers to be made between the monitor and the virtual machine.

Each VP/ix virtual DOS machine is simply a single UNIX process containing two separate tasks (see Figure A-3): a V8086 task that runs in the first megabyte of the user's virtual address space and a monitor task that runs in 32-bit protected mode just above that. The user-level monitor task is called the Emulation Control Task, or ECT.

The two tasks trade off control as follows. When the VP/ix process is initialized, the ECT loads a modified 80286 BIOS into the virtual 8086 from a UNIX disk file, then performs a task switch and starts executing the BIOS initialization code in V8086 mode. Whenever a trap out of the V8086 task takes place, a "mini-monitor" in the kernel quickly examines the cause of the trap and either:

- handles the exception itself and returns to the user level in V8086 mode, or
- immediately returns to user mode, but in the ECT, rather than in the V8086 task, so that the ECT can handle the exception.

The kernel mini-monitor handles only the most time-critical exceptions. In particular, all code with any DOS or BIOS-related knowledge resides at the user level rather than in the kernel. Hardware device emulations, meanwhile, are handled both by the ECT and (modified) UNIX device drivers.

Code inside the V8086 task that knows it's running under VP/ix (the special VP/ix BIOS, for instance) can trap directly into the ECT without going through the kernel at all. The ECT always returns to the V8086 task directly, with no kernel intervention. A surprisingly small number of modifications to the kernel have made it possible for UNIX to "understand" that a single process could, in fact, contain two tasks.

Eventually, the BIOS (with help from the ECT) loads DOS into the virtual 8086 from another UNIX disk file, and the virtual PC is off and running. At these times, the machine usually is doing one of two things: accessing files or writing to screen. We now will examine how VP/ix handles these tasks.

Emulation of the DOS File System

Client DOS applications under VP/ix can use files stored in the UNIX file system, on a DOS diskette, or on a DOS disk partition. As a rule, the UNIX file system suffices for all DOS file storage; no DOS hard disk partition is required, and usually none is present. This means that most file accesses done by DOS programs must be transformed invisibly into equivalent UNIX file-system operations.

Redirection

As part of virtual machine initialization, a special DOS "terminate-and-stay-resident" program called a "redirector" is placed into the virtual 8086 part of each virtual DOS machine. This program creates one or more new DOS "pseudo-drives" that correspond to nodes in the UNIX file system. Whenever a DOS program makes a request involving one of the pseudo-drives, the redirector intercepts the DOS system calls and redirects them to a UNIX "agent" for processing. In the case of VP/ix, this agent is the Emulation Control Task. In other implementations, it's a separate file server process.

For example, the user might choose to make drive **U:** be the DOS equivalent of a UNIX directory called **/usr/joe/dosprogs**. Thereafter, whenever the user lists the DOS drive **U:** directory, all the file names in that UNIX directory will be displayed in DOS format. What that actually means is that the redirector will send the DOS directory-scanning requests to the ECT, which then will scan the corresponding UNIX directory and send matching file names back to the redirector, which in turn will send them on to DOS for display on the screen—in DOS format.

UNIX file system ownership and permissions are respected throughout this entire process; each virtual DOS environment looks to the rest of UNIX like an ordinary process with the access privileges of the DOS user. If a DOS file access fails because of UNIX permission problems, the redirector will return a DOS error code that approximates the error code UNIX returned to the file server task (or process). For example, if a DOS program attempts to write into a directory without the proper write permission, the UNIX **EACCES** error would appear to the DOS program as a DOS "ACCESS DENIED" error.

Record locking via DOS function 5C is translated into UNIX file locking using the **lockf()** system call, but only if the DOS application issues the lock. It isn't possible to detect or resolve certain kinds of file conflicts among multiple DOS users. For example, if two DOS users are working on spreadsheets at the same time and are imprudent enough not only to pick the same name for their spreadsheet file but also to save their files in the same directory, the user who saves his or her work last will "win" by virtue of overwriting the other's spreadsheet. DOS-under-UNIX users, like all other UNIX users, must simply be warned that this condition exists, and be told that they must either keep their work in private directories or use application programs that perform explicit record-locking.

File Names

Giving DOS programs access to the UNIX file system raises an interesting question: which UNIX file names should satisfy a DOS directory scanning request?

After all, UNIX and DOS file-naming conventions are quite different. DOS file names can be up to 11 characters in length, of which the last three, if present, can only be used as an "extension." DOS names, moreover, are case-insensitive and cannot contain the same special characters UNIX names can. By contrast, UNIX file names can be 14 characters in length, are case sensitive, and can contain, for example, more than one period. There are, therefore, many more UNIX file name possibilities than there are potential DOS file names. How, then, should UNIX file names be represented when listing a UNIX directory from within DOS?

Two different approaches are possible. In the first, all UNIX file names that can't be directly translated to DOS simply aren't reported to the redirector and therefore are made invisible to DOS programs. Any file whose UNIX name contains more than 11 characters, or has more than three characters following a period, or that includes upper-case letters, or harbors unacceptable special characters doesn't appear in the DOS directory listing and can't be accessed by a DOS application.

In the second approach, an algorithm is applied to each nonconforming UNIX file name to "map it down" to an acceptable DOS name before reporting it to the redirector. Special characters generally are used by such algorithms to make the names unlikely to clash with "real" DOS file names; for example, the UNIX file *my.unix.file* might show up in a DOS directory listing as *MY~UN~AA.FI~*.

Imagine comparing a DOS listing and a UNIX listing of the same UNIX directory. If the first approach were used to generate the DOS listing, the number of lines in the two listings would often be different, with the DOS listing containing fewer lines. With the second approach, the line count would always be the same, but some of the file names in one listing would be different from those in the other. The first approach is simpler, but less informative. The second is more informative, but can also be more confusing.

After some discussion, some prototyping, and some fisticuffs, we at Interactive Systems decided to use the second approach in VP/ix. The same approach is used in Locus Computing's Merge 386. Thus the Emulation Control Task or DOS server process transforms UNIX file names as described above before reporting them to the redirector in the virtual 8086 task. Some other products that store DOS files in the UNIX file system—most notably such DOS/UNIX networking products as Xenix Net and Vianet—use the simpler "disappearing file name" approach.

Emulation of the DOS Display

Because all 80386 systems are potentially multi-user machines, a viable DOS-under-UNIX system for the 80386 must allow users who are logged in either on the system console or a serial terminal to run DOS applications. Currently, systems have at most one console display device that's compatible with a PC AT graphics adapter; the second and subsequent users log in on serial terminals. (Happily, advances in technology are alleviating this restriction. For example, VP/ix supports SunRiver Corporation's Cygna FiberStation, a very high-speed, high-resolution graphics terminal that allows several users to run DOS graphics applications at the same time.)

A UNIX user who's logged in on an ordinary serial terminal (a VT100 or TVI925, for example) can run any DOS program that doesn't require a graphics adapter. This doesn't reduce the number of available applications by much since most popular DOS applications will take advantage of graphics facilities if they're present, but also will run on the IBM Monochrome Display Adapter (or MDA), which is a character-only video controller. All of the major spreadsheets and word processors, and most of the important database managers run on the MDA, and therefore work well on serial terminals running under UNIX.

DOS display handling is the most common example of "ill-behavior" found in these applications. The BIOS and, to a lesser extent, DOS have system-call interfaces meant to let applications send characters and graphics to the display. However, these interfaces are considered too slow by PC experts, and therefore popular DOS applications almost universally ignore them. Instead, DOS implementors take advantage of the fact that their applications run alone in an unprotected hardware environment and write directly to video memory and display controllers, bypassing DOS and BIOS entirely (and, it must be granted, achieving snappier video performance as a result).

On the console of a PC-compatible machine, the slowness of the DOS and BIOS interfaces can be sidestepped by giving an application direct access to display hardware. Some special facilities in the kernel likewise allow the V8086 monitor to map the real-screen buffer into the proper location in the virtual PC's address space, as well as to give the DOS program access to the display controller's I/O registers (but to no others—selective I/O permission, after all, poses no threat to system integrity). As a result, all DOS graphics applications work properly, including such heinously ill-behaved programs as Microsoft Flight Simulator and various arcade-game adaptations.

However, when running on a serial terminal, no shortcuts are possible. It's hard to persuade a program that it should modify its behavior just because the display is located on the other end of an RS-232 cable (programs that already have been sold to 2 million customers are especially hard to convince). DOS-under-UNIX facilities must make the RS-232 connection invisible for these programs by completely emulating the MDA.

There are four separate issues that must be dealt with to emulate the MDA completely on an arbitrary terminal. The implementation details, once again, are taken directly from VP/ix, but essentially similar approaches are to be found in all products.

Video Buffer Emulation

As mentioned above, the liberties that DOS applications take in the way of direct access to video refresh buffer constitute by far and away the most common form of "ill behavior." Programs write into memory locations which they assume correspond to screen locations. This correspondence must be maintained in a virtual machine so that when a DOS application writes a character to a location in its "screen buffer," that character will be reflected on the terminal screen serving as the DOS display.

In addition, DOS applications that employ "pop-up" user interfaces must *read* from the screen as well as write to it if they are to redisplay the text that's been obscured by pop-up events. Programs that allow cutting and pasting of text from one window to another must also be able to read data from the video buffer. It's not enough, therefore, for a monitor to intercept a write to the screen and send the character to a terminal; the entire display adapter video buffer must be completely emulated.

VP/ix deals with this problem as follows. The ECT maps an area of ordinary virtual memory at the screen buffer address (hex A0000) that corresponds to each virtual PC running on a terminal. A DOS application will treat this memory as its video buffer, writing to it to display data on the screen, and reading from it to recover displayed text. This "pseudo-video" memory is *not* illegal or unwritable in any way; the DOS program can read and write it at top speed without causing a trap. However, the ECT does inform the kernel that it wishes to be notified whenever the contents of this memory location are changed.

The kernel determines whether the pseudo-video buffer has changed by periodically (at every 100 Hz—the UNIX clock interval) examining the buffer's hardware-maintained "page modified" bit. Whenever this bit is set, the kernel knows the DOS program has altered video memory, and it notifies the ECT accordingly. The ECT then analyzes the pseudo-video buffer to determine what has changed (with a very quick assembly language routine), and—via the standard UNIX **tty** driver—sends to the terminal the smallest data stream needed to synchronize the terminal display with the buffer. UNIX **terminfo** data (plus some extra information described below) is used to determine the most efficient way to update the terminal. For example, if the ECT detects a vertical scroll in the video buffer, it updates the screen by sending only a newline character and the bottom line of text.

We found during the prototyping of VP/ix that this method performed much better than the alternative, which was to trap every write to video memory and immediately duplicate it on the terminal. The pseudo-video approach provides good screen response for several DOS users, and it also works well with all the standard DOS pop-up programs.

Output Character Mapping

The MDA has an extended character set that most DOS programs use heavily. The extended set includes box-drawing characters, "smiley" faces, musical notes, foreign letters, and the like. There are a few new terminals on the market, from companies including Wyse and Kimtron, that are able to display the entire IBM character set. But, though these are excellent for use with DOS-under-UNIX systems, they still make up only a small portion of the overall installed base. Most terminals can't display the extra IBM characters, so characters from each terminal's more restricted character set must be substituted. The different screen attributes of the MDA (underline, bold, blinking, reverse) in various combinations must also be substituted for when possible.

The substitution mechanism must be flexible not only because different terminals have different character sets, but also because different users may prefer different substitutions even on the same terminal.

VP/ix solves this problem with a fairly simple ASCII terminal configuration file that the ECT digests into a memory-based table during VP/ix initialization. For each terminal type, there's a separate configuration file, which lists the mappings between IBM PC characters and the attributes and native character set of the terminal in question. The ECT uses this table to translate each character before sending it to the terminal.

A standard set of configuration files is supplied with VP/ix, but each user may tailor one or more of them to his own taste by editing a copy of a default file, then pointing to the new file with an environment variable.

Keyboard Input Mapping

A similar mapping problem exists for keyboard input, because most terminal keyboards don't match the keyboard of the PC AT. A separate section of the terminal configuration file therefore controls keystroke mapping. The problem is that while one terminal might have a "Control" key, several others will have "Alt" keys, "PgUp/PgDn" keys, and the like. Unfortunately, many PC applications have complex keyboard-based user interfaces in which every possible combination of keys is assigned a meaning. Therefore, a DOS-under-UNIX system must be able to deliver every possible combination of IBM PC keys to a DOS application, regardless of the number of keys a given terminal keyboard affords.

There's yet another complication as well. The keyboard of a serial terminal transmits the ASCII values of the keys pressed, and—in the case of special keys such as function keys—sequences of ASCII characters may be transmitted. PC keyboards, on the other hand, transmit numerical values called "scan codes" that correspond to the position a key occupies on the keyboard. Furthermore, a separate scan code is transmitted when a key is depressed, followed by another when the key is released (these are called "make" and "break" codes, respectively). Thus, there must be a mapping between the ASCII characters sent out by the terminal and the sequence of scan codes a PC application expects to receive.

For example, the ASCII "a" key, when shifted, transmits (octal) 101, the ASCII code for "A." However, a PC application expects to see the (hex) scan codes 2A, 1E, 9E, and AA—in that order—corresponding to the make code for the shift key, the make and break codes for the "a" key, and the break code for the shift key.

There are a number of keys on a PC keyboard, moreover, that don't correspond to any ASCII character whatsoever; among these are the PC's ten function keys, its three toggle keys (caps lock, num lock, scroll lock), the keys on its numerical keypad, and the ctrl, left shift, and right shift keys. These last three, while present on ASCII keyboards, don't transmit a character, but instead modify characters transmitted by other keys. In order to communicate with PC applications, then, it must be possible to "tell" DOS that each of these keys has been pressed. In fact, some applications need to know separately when "Alt" and "Shift" keys have been pressed (make code), and when they've been released (break code).

To handle all possible cases, input-control lines in the VP/ix terminal configuration file allow for arbitrary mappings between sequences of input ASCII characters and sequences of scan codes. The ECT reads ASCII characters from the UNIX **tty** driver, expands them into scan codes as directed by the configuration file, and finally feeds the scan codes into the BIOS one at a time to provide emulated PC keyboard input to the DOS virtual machine.

The 24-line Problem

For the most part, older terminals can display only 24 lines of text. All standard PC displays have 25 lines, and every popular PC application uses all 25 of them. Many newer terminals have 25 lines, but no OEM customer would buy a DOS-under-UNIX system unable to support the installed terminal base. To provide general PC display emulation on serial terminals, therefore, a mildly annoying bullet has to be bitten: 24-line terminals have to be made to emulate 25-line DOS displays.

VP/ix addresses this problem by defining a "rocker" key in the terminal control file. By default, the 24 lines of a terminal correspond to the bottom 24 lines of a DOS display. That means the top line isn't visible on the screen, but it's present in the pseudo-display buffer. By pressing the rocker key, the user can bring the display down one line, such that it shows the top, rather than the bottom, 24 lines. The rocking action is quick, because the ECT uses the terminal's insert/delete line capabilities to handle most of the screen movement work right at the terminal.

Actually, this technique isn't nearly as bad as it sounds. We've found, in fact, that users get used to it rather quickly; the slight annoyance of having to use a rocker key is more than made up for by the pleasure of being able to run a wide range of DOS applications on an old terminal.

B

Where to Buy

We've mentioned many different products in the course of this book. By now, you're probably wondering where you can get them. Products such as PC-Interface, Merge and VP/ix are sold on an OEM basis, and are available from multiple sources. In such cases, we've listed as a principal contact the developer of the product (e.g., Locus Computing for Merge and PC-Interface) and listed only the names (not addresses and phone numbers) of resellers of the product.

While we've tried to make this appendix as complete as possible, there are many products out there. If your company produces a product that you feel should be included, please let us know, and we'll try to work it into the next edition.

For ease of reference, this appendix is divided into the following sections:

- **Dual Environments**—Merge, MKS Toolkit, SoftPC, Sun IPC, VP/ix
- **Networking Products**—PC/TCP, PC-Interface, PC-NFS, TERM, Vianet and XenixNet
- **Terminals**—PC-scancode and memory-mapped
- **UNIX Implementations** for Generic 386 Machines

Within each category, products are listed in alphabetical order.

Dual Environments

Merge 286 and Merge 386

Locus Computing Corp.
3330 Ocean Park Blvd.
Santa Monica, CA 90405
(213) 452-2435

Merge is available on systems from the following vendors:

- AT&T (under the name Simultask, for 286-based systems)
- Convergent
- Microport Systems
- Prime
- Unisys

VP/ix

Interactive Systems
2401 Colorado Avenue, 3rd Floor
Santa Monica, CA 90404
(213) 453-8649

VP/ix is sold with both the Xenix and 386/ix generic UNIX implementations for the 386. Contact Interactive for a list of distributors, as well as the 386 machines that have been tested and found compatible with VP/ix. VP/ix is also sold by AT&T under the name Simultask 386.

MKS Toolkit

Mortice Kern Systems, Inc.
43 Bridgeport Road East
Waterloo, Ontario
Canada N2J2J4
(519) 884-2251

This is a terrific collection of utilities that bring UNIX functionality to DOS systems. It contains well over 100 UNIX utilities, including **vi**, **sed**, and **awk**.

SoftPC

Insignia Solutions
1255 Post Street, Suite 625
San Francisco, CA 94109
(415) 885-4455

This product is available for the Apple Macintosh II running either the MAC OS or A/UX and for a number of popular UNIX workstations.

SUN IPC

Sun Microsystems
Two Federal Street
Billerica, MA 01821
(617) 667-0010

Networking Products

PC-Interface

Locus Computing Corp.
3330 Ocean Park Blvd.
Santa Monica, CA 90405
(213) 452-2435

PC-Interface is available on systems from the following vendors:

- Counterpoint (S19)
- AT&T (3B2 and 3B15)
- Convergent (Miniframe or Mightyframe)
- DEC (MicroVAX or VAX running Ultrix or 4.3 BSD)
- Honeywell (SGM2)
- Motorola (S8000)
- NCR (Tower series)
- Prime (EXL-316)
- Ridge (Model 32)
- Unisys (Tower, Arete, or CCI systems)

PC-NFS

Sun Microsystems
Two Federal Street
Billerica, MA 01821
(617) 667-0010

PC/TCP

FTP Software
PO BOX 150
Kendall Square Branch
Boston, MA 02142
(617) 868-4878

TERM

Century Software
5284 South 320 West, Suite C294
Salt Lake City, UT 84107
(801) 268-3088

ViaNet

Western Digital Corp.
2445 McCabe Way
Irvine, CA 92714
(800) NET-LEADER (800-638-5323)

XenixNet

Originally developed by Microsoft, this product is available from a number of resellers, including Altos, Compaq, IBM and Tandy. It is available direct to end users from:

The Santa Cruz Operation
400 Encinal Street
PO Box 1900
Santa Cruz, CA 95061
(800) 626-UNIX (800-626-8649)
(408) 425-7222

Terminals and Serial Expansion Boards

Memory-Mapped Terminals

Cygna 386 Fiber Optic Station

Sun River Corporation
PO Box 9367
Jackson, MS 39206
(601) 957-0100

Scancode Terminals

Almost every terminal manufacturer now offers at least one PC-scancode terminal (sometimes called PC-Term emulation). Here are three we've seen advertised recently.

Esprit PCT4, Opus 3n1

Esprit Systems, Inc.
100 Marcus Drive
Melville, NY 11747
(800) 645-4508
(516) 293-5600

Televideo 965

Televideo Systems
1170 Morse Avenue
Sunnyvale, CA 94088
(800) 835-3228

Wyse 60

Wyse Technology
3571 First Street
San Jose, CA 95134
(408) 433-1000

Serial Expansion Boards

Serial expansion boards are needed with scancode terminals, but not memory-mapped terminals. Here are two vendors we know of:

Arnet Corp.
618 Grassmere Park Drive, Suite 6
Nashville, TN 37211
(800) 366-8844

DigiBoard
6751 Oxford Street
St. Louis Park, MN 55426
(612) 922-8055

UNIX Implementations for Generic 386 Machines

386/ix

Interactive Systems Corp.
2401 Colorado Avenue, 3rd Floor
Santa Monica, CA 90404
(213) 453-8649

GNU

GNU (GNU is Not UNIX) is a freeware implementation of a UNIX lookalike. It is still under development, but portions of it (including many utilities that can be compiled under DOS as well as UNIX) are available from:

The Free Software Foundation
675 Massachusetts Avenue
Cambridge, MA 02139
(617) 876-3296

Microport System V/386

Microport Systems
10 Victor Square
Scotts Valley, CA 95066
(408) 438-8649

Xenix

The Santa Cruz Operation
400 Encinal Street
PO Box 1900
Santa Cruz, CA 95061
(800) 626-UNIX (800-626-8649)
(408) 425-7222

Xenix is also available direct from Altos, Compaq, IBM, and others.

GLOSSARY

ASCII terminal—A terminal whose keyboard generates ASCII (American Standard Code for Information Interchange) codes, and whose screen displays characters when it receives such a code. ASCII terminals are commonly used with UNIX systems. (See also **scancode terminal**.)

background process—A program that is still running, but which no longer requires interaction from the user, and has returned the user to the shell prompt so he or she can run another program.

A background process can be actively working, or can be suspended temporarily. UNIX allows users to put any **stream-oriented program** into the background while it is running, and to suspend any **display-oriented program**. Background processes are an important aspect of any **multi-tasking** system, although they are less important on a system that supports **windowing**.

bandwidth—The total amount of information-carrying capacity of a communications link. The effective capacity of a link may be less than its full bandwidth. For example, an Ethernet transfers data at a rate of 10 megabits (million bits per second), but network overhead may use up more than half of this. The remainder must be shared between all devices on the network. An RS-232 serial link, on the other hand, may run at only 9600 bps (bits per second), but it is all available for communication between the terminal and the host. (Ethernet is still *much* faster, but not by as large a margin as you might expect from the raw bandwidth.)

client —In a local area network, any system that makes use of network services. In many networks containing both DOS and UNIX systems, a DOS system can only act as a client, not as a **server**.

command—A directive to the computer. Application programs (such as 123) typically have their own internal commands. As used in this book, the term refers to either an *internal command*, which is built into the **command interpreter**, or an *external command*, which corresponds to the name of an executable program. External commands are must be located in a directory defined as a part of the user's **search path**.

command interpreter—The program that manages the interaction with the user, interpreting any commands, options and filenames typed in. The UNIX command interpreter is called the **shell**; the DOS command interpreter is called *command.com*.

current directory—The **directory** in a hierarchical file system in which the user is "located" and on which all file operations will take place unless a **pathname** is used to specify a different location for the operation.

departmental computer system— A multi-user computer system that serves as a hub in a local area network. This network can be extended vertically by connections to mainframe computers or personal computers and horizontally by connections to other departmental-level computer systems. The departmental computer acts like a supervisor, managing and overseeing resources and operations common to all users.

directory—A special kind of file that appears to "contain" other files and directories. A convenient way of organizing files on a large disk. The complete set of files and directories makes up a **file system**.

disk partition—a section of a computer's hard disk that is has its own separate disk formatting information. A DOS disk may be partitioned so that it appears to the user as two disk drives (e.g. C: and D:). A UNIX disk can be partitioned into separate **file systems**. It is also possible to format a disk such that it has separate partitions for DOS and UNIX.

display-oriented program—A program that interacts with the user by taking over the computer display and keyboard. Such a program can typically not write data to a pipe nor have its output redirected to a file. Most DOS applications are display-oriented, as are some UNIX programs, such as the *vi* screen editor. (See **stream-oriented program**.)

Ethernet—A high speed **local area network**.

file server—A system that allows other members of a **local area network** to use its disk to store files.

file system—The means by which a computer system organizes data for access by users. Both DOS and UNIX support a hierarchical file system, in which files are stored in directories, and directories in other directories, until all can be seen to be contained in a primordial "root directory." However, the actual data structures by which the user view of files and directories are mapped onto the physical disk are very different between DOS and UNIX.

local area network—A high-speed link between systems that allows them to transfer files, or to use another system as a **file** or **print server**. A network that allows systems to act both as **clients** and **servers** to each other is sometimes called a peer network.

pipe—A method for passing data (a stream of bytes) between two programs.

print server—A system that allows other members of a **local area network** to access its printer.

scancode terminal—A terminal whose keyboard can produce PC-compatible scan codes instead of (or as well as) ASCII codes, and whose 25-line screen can display the PC's extended ASCII graphic character set. PC keyboards produce separate codes (make and break codes) when a key is depressed and when it is released.

server—A system on a local area network that allows other systems (**clients**) to access its disk, printer, or other devices. In a peer network, systems can act as servers for each other.

stream-oriented program—A program that expects a stream of ASCII bytes as input, and produces a similar stream as output. Input can come from the keyboard, from a file, or from a **pipe**. Output can go to the screen, into a pipe, or be redirected to a file. DOS programs like DIR, TYPE, and MORE are stream-oriented, as are most UNIX programs.

pathname—A method of indicating a file's place in a hierarchical **file system** by showing the directories that must be traversed to reach it. An absolute pathname shows the sequence of directories between the root directory of the file system and the file. A relative pathname shows the sequence of directories between the **current directory** and the file.

search path—The sequence of directories the **command interpreter** should look through to find the executable file corresponding to a **command**.

virtual memory—A memory-addressing scheme in which processes read from and write to arbitrary locations in a memory space that is much larger than the machine's actual physical memory. Special memory-mapping hardware in the CPU translates these virtual memory addresses to real addresses, keeping most-frequently used data in physical memory, and swapping the data out to disk if necessary. Virtual memory is essential for high performance on a multi-user, multi-tasking system. Both the Motorola 68010 and 68020 support virtual memory, which is why they've been the preferred processor for most UNIX **workstations**. The 80386 is the first Intel processor to support virtual memory.

virtual PC—A term used (by analogy with **virtual memory**) for an environment such as Merge or VP/ix. These products use the 80386's virtual memory and a special "virtual-8086" processor mode to give DOS programs the illusion that they are running on a single-user PC, in complete control of the hardware, when in fact they are sharing the resources of a multi-user system.

windowing—A method for dividing a computer screen into multiple independent areas. Windows can be used simply to organize data on the screen, as on the Macintosh, or with some PC environments. On a multi-tasking system, they can allow the user to work with multiple concurrent tasks.

workstation—A high-performance computer with a graphics screen and a **windowing** environment. Even though most workstations use the multi-user UNIX operating system, they are often dedicated to a single user. Workstations are often connected over a **local area network**, and diskless workstations, whose only file storage is accessible over the network, are fairly common.

High-end workstations cost $20,000 or even more. However, recent product introductions from Sun Microsystems have brought the price down to near-PC prices for low-end workstations. Apple's new Macintosh II with A/UX will help to continue this trend.

Index

A

B

C

D

E

K

L

M

N

O

P

Q

R

S

V

W

X

Colophon

Our look is the result of reader comments, our own experimentation, and distribution channels.

Distinctive covers complement our distinctive approach to UNIX documentation, breathing personality and life into potentially dry subjects. UNIX and its attendant programs can be unruly beasts. Nutshell Handbooks help you tame them.

The animals featured on the front cover of *DOS Meets UNIX* are a squirrel monkey and a horned owl.

Edie Freedman designed this cover and the entire UNIX bestiary that appears on other Nutshell Handbooks. The beasts themselves are adapted from 19th-century engravings from the Dover Pictorial Archive.

Linda Lamb designed the page layout for the Nutshell Handbooks. The text of this book is set in Times Roman; headings are Helvetica®; examples are Courier. Text was prepared using SoftQuad's *sqtroff* text formatter. Figures are produced with a Macintosh™. Printing is done on an Apple LaserWriter®.

Overseas Distributors

Effective January 1, 1990, customers outside the U.S. and Canada will be able to order Nutshell Handbooks and the X Window System Series through distributors near them. These overseas locations offer international customers faster order processing, more local bookstores and local distributors, an increased representation at trade shows worldwide, as well as the high level, quality service our customers have always received.

AUSTRALIA & NEW ZEALAND
(orders and inquiries)
Addison-Wesley Publishers, Pty. Ltd.
6 Byfield Street
North Ryde, N.S.W. 2113
AUSTRALIA
Telephone: 61-2-888-2733
FAX: 61-2-888-9404

UNITED KINGDOM & AFRICA
(orders and inquiries)
Addison-Wesley Publishers, Ltd.
Finchampstead Road
Wokingham, Berkshire RG11 2NZ
U.S.A.
ENGLAND
Telephone: 44-734-794-000
FAX: 44-734-794-035

EUROPE & THE MIDDLE EAST
(orders and inquiries)
Addison-Wesley Publishers B.V.
De Lairessestraat 90
1071 PJ Amsterdam
THE NETHERLANDS
Telephone: 31-20-764-044
FAX: 31-20-664-5334

ASIA inquiries (excluding Japan)
Addison-Wesley Singapore Pte. Ltd.
15 Beach Road #05-09/10
Beach Centre
Singapore 0718
SINGAPORE
Telephone: 65-339-7503
FAX: 65-339-9709

ASIA orders (excluding Japan)
Addison-Wesley Publishing Co., Inc.
International Order Department
Route 128
Reading, Massachusetts 01867

Telephone: 1-617-944-3700
FAX: 1-617-942-2829

JAPAN
(orders and inquiries)
Toppan Company, Ltd.
Ochanomizu Square B, 1-6
Kanda Surugadai
Chiyoda-ku, Tokyo 101
JAPAN
Telephone: 81-3-295-3461
FAX: 81-3-293-5963